I BELIEVE IN SANTA CLAUS AND I BELIEVE IN GOD

I BELIEVE IN SANTA CLAUS AND I BELIEVE IN GOD

Why I Believe

By J. Lynn Currie

ARPress

ILLUMINATING IDEAS
EMPOWERING VOICES

ARPress
45 Dan Road Suite 5
Canton MA 02021
Hotline: 1(888) 821-0229
Fax: 1(508) 545-7580

Ordering Information:
Quantity sales. Special discounts are available on quantity purchases by corporations, associations, and others. For details, contact the publisher at the address above.

Printed in the United States of America.

ISBN-13:   Softcover   979-8-89330-473-2
           eBook   979-8-89330-474-9

Library of Congress Control Number: 2024901849

Biblical quotes are from the New Jerusalem Bible unless otherwise noted.

Definitions are from the Concise Oxford American Dictionary (2006) unless otherwise noted.

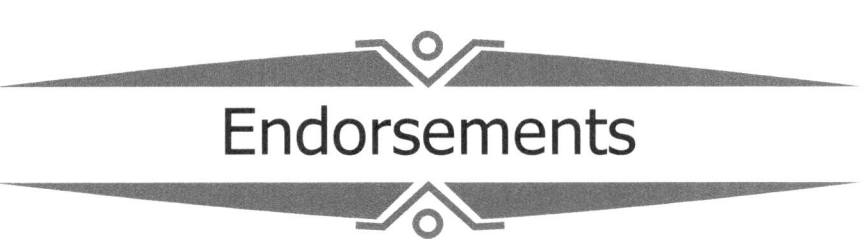

Endorsements

I've known Lynn for around 20 years. Some of us call him a deep thinker. I know he has passion about his belief and the material he covers in this book. It is a worthy read for anyone with doubts about their faith because of science or philosophy. I would share this book with anyone having those struggles or others to bolster their belief. Reverend Don Coventry, Deacon. St. John's Episcopal Church, Decatur, IL. Detective (Retired), Decatur Police Department, Decatur, IL.

I met Lynn 45 years ago when I was a second-year medical student. For 5 years our families met weekly in a small group Bible study. What wonderful memories as "iron sharpened iron." Lynn's wit, candor, insight and love of Jesus shined brightly then as it does in this book. Have a highlighter ready as you read this … you might just wear it out. Dennis E. McCreary, M.D. American Board of Family Medicine certified. Family Medicine, Aurora Health Care, Zion, IL. Associate Clinical Professor, Chicago Medical School.

I met Lynn when we were working in the same Division of a State agency. His writing skills were well known. As I was then, and still am, also a preacher, we connected. Over the years we've had many conversations of a theological and philosophical nature. In this book, he does a good job of sharing his reasons for believing in God. The material is straightforward, though he does emphasize those areas that are of greater importance to him. I would recommend this book to anyone who doesn't believe or may have trouble believing because of the issues discussed. Reverend Donald Peck, Pastor, Loami United Methodist Church, Loami, IL.

Lynn is the first person I baptized into Christ. He was 14 and I was his 19-year-old youth minister. Lynn's faith was vibrant and enthusiastic. I still remember his response after reading *Tortured for Christ* by Richard Wurmbrand, a book I gave him to read. When he returned it, his reaction shocked me. He said something to the effect, "I wish I could be there. It really costs you something to believe in Christ when facing persecution."

The trials Lynn faced in life can't be characterized as persecution, but they were enough to test his faith. In fact, they destroyed it...for a time. But after lying dormant through a life of physical, emotional, and spiritual struggles, the seeds of faith that were planted in his youth came back to life, and what you read here gives evidence to his not only renewed but deepened and even more robust faith in Christ.

If life has challenged your faith in a God who not only exists but loves you and cared enough to send His Son to die for you, let Lynn's journey through the minefields of life offer some help and direction that may very well enable you to reach the promised shore. Rick Wenneborg, Minister. Chatham Christian Church, Chatham, IL.

Preface

When I was around eleven years old, I was rather crudely and laughingly told that I was too old to believe in Santa Claus. Years later, I was often told that I was too old and too smart to believe in God. I take exception to both of those declarations.

The Santa Claus thing is no big deal. But my belief in God is a big deal to me. Some people find my belief irrational, unscientific, delusional, or even dangerous. I don't think so.

I believe that it makes every bit as much sense to believe in God as to not believe in God. I mean that in terms of logic, philosophy, science, and common sense.

It's often difficult to have a serious discussion with any one about anything. I've found it particularly so when trying to share with family, friends, or acquaintances the reasons why I believe in God. There are a number of reasons why I believe in God. Outside of the difficulty of sharing all or most of them in any casual conversation, it is the combination of the reasons (which I also refer to as evidence) all together, with faith, that support my choice to believe. In this regard, it is like the principle wherein the whole is greater than the sum of the parts.

Say, a friend tells you he was at the "SOD BAR" last night. You doubt him. He says he was there between about 10:00 p.m. and midnight. He was with a friend. That friend says they were there. But that could be collusion. The bartender recognizes a picture of your friend but can't be sure of what day or time he last saw him. A patron thinks she remembers seeing someone in the rather interesting shirt he was wearing. The security camera has a picture of a car that looks like your friend's but not of your friend. Do you believe your friend more or less? Part of your decision will be based on the evidence and your belief in your friend. Dog gone. *Life is a **S**trange **O**ld **D**og.* [Phrase taken from a line in the series Providence.]

In this little book I attempt to share my reasons for believing in God. I hope that I do so in a way that you can understand where I'm coming from, whether you agree or not.

Acknowledgements

I first, want to say thanks to Rick Wenneborg, who shepherded me in to the faith and has been a friend, mentor and encourager in my life and my writing. I also thank Lynn Laughlin, who taught the first psychology course I took. As the Dean of Students, he also demonstrated to me the grace of God in my life experience. My long-time friend, Jim Clarkson, read and discussed my writing with me. As far as I know, he's not a theist but his comments helped me refine presentation of some of my thoughts. My daughter, Jackie, discussed some of the content and made me pay attention to my punctuation, as well as asking how it was going. Susan, my wife, has supported me throughout the process. I thank her for her encouragement even if it was often something like, if you're going to do it, then do it. And, most of all, I give thanks to God, the Great Spirit, who I believe in some way encouraged a thought that this might be worth doing.

Contents

INTRODUCTION

When someone tells me that they don't believe in God, I usually just say that I do. Generally, they'll ask me why. This tends to lead to at least a little discussion. I start to respond by saying something like the following. It seems to me that either matter has always existed or God has always existed and is the cause, the creator of the matter that exists. Then the conversation goes here or there and sometimes nowhere at all.

I don't want to and don't think it'd be right to impose my beliefs on others, even if I could. However, as a Christian theist I always hope to share some reason for others to consider the plausibility of the existence of God.

You can't prove the existence of God. As far as I know, that is true. And, as far as I know, you can't prove that God doesn't exist. On the one hand, you can't prove that something that doesn't exist doesn't exist. On the other hand, you can prove the existence of something that exists if you have adequate understanding, information, and ability to test related hypotheses.

In the scientific realm there are numerous things that are believed to exist or work in certain ways based on plausible hypotheses. But an unproven hypothesis is still just a hypothesis, whether it is believed or not. If a person believes (or believes in) anything that is hypothetical or theoretical, that is an act of faith. One way to think about the difference is that no one asks or is asked if they believe in water. Water is a compound of hydrogen and oxygen (H_2O) and everyone knows that it is real. Something like ghosts is a different story, whether you enjoy Ghostbusters or not.

In order to prove that something exists, that something must be a thing. It must be something that in some way is identifiable and measurable. Indulge me for a moment to be abstract and theological in this regard. Is God something? By most, if not all, theologies God is considered to be spirit. Spirit could be considered a thing, but a thing that is beyond our ability to scientifically examine.

I believe that there is a whole lot about the spiritual world (let alone the material world we see) that we don't know. For example, I believe there is good evidence for ESP, extrasensory perception, in different ways. In Christian theology, God created many spirit beings, or entities, some of which were angels. Some angels rebelled and ended being what we call demons. Something like demons or other spiritual entities may take human form or some form that could be scientifically detectable and studied. Maybe what we call ghosts are detectable. In the past, the word ghost was interchangeable with spirit, as in the Holy Ghost or Holy Spirit. Ghosts may or may not be the spirit of a dead person. Whatever, such an apparition may be physically detectable. I don't know, just not ruling it out. It just doesn't matter to me.

If we assume that God is spirit and has the characteristics and nature attributed Him by Christianity, we could never imagine that we could prove his existence. From a Christian perspective this includes and requires faith. Not a blind leap of faith, but faith in the context of evidence and experience.

In a court of law, jurors are instructed to find a defendant guilty if they find it so beyond a reasonable doubt. Not absolute doubt. Very few things are without a possible trace of doubt after all. I hope that you might find believing in God reasonable, even with reasonable doubts. Don't we put our trust in many things even with reasonable doubts? We trust the plane will fly. Yet, there are definite odds as to the probability that we will crash. With that scientific reasonable doubt, we risk our lives every time we fly. I admit that is a bad analogy, but I'm trying to say that some things are reasonable to believe in even with some doubts.

Generally, when we talk to someone, we like to believe that we share some common ground. Such isn't always the case. I like to think

I'm a fairly tolerant person but I don't have much for someone who doesn't believe in reality. I mean, if you don't believe in reality, then the whole conversation is unreal, right? I believe in absolutes and reality is one of them. Someone might say that I believe in God and that's my reality but it's not theirs. Well, we all live in the same reality whether we believe different things or not. Yes, we do perceive reality differently to a greater or lesser extent, but that doesn't mean there are different realities that we are perceiving.

Sometimes my wife will say it's hot, while I'm feeling chilly. The temperature is the same. Doesn't mean that she's not feeling hot or that I'm not feeling chilly. The thermometer doesn't register a different temperature for each of us. Nor does it show a feels-like temperature for each of us.

Some say that everything is relative. That's relatively true. But a thing is only relative to something else. If there were only one temperature, there would not be any hotter or colder. Yet, that wouldn't prevent the wife from feeling warmer or me cooler. The way people use the term "relative" makes me think that if everything is relative then the statement that everything is relative is relative.

The theory of relativity has primarily to do with perspective. Simply, that the perspective of an observer changes the perception of the observer. Hence, the speed of a moving object can be perceived differently depending on the perspective of the observer. Scientifically accepted and demonstrable.

The theory of relativity has been applied to psychology, sociology, philosophy, and morality in the extreme. To the point as to say that there is ultimately no (absolute) truth or right and wrong; there is only one's perception of it. Regardless of our ideas of truth or right and wrong, which may be quite different, everybody has some concept of truth and right and wrong. Can you imagine anyone not agreeing with the statement that it's not right for you to do me wrong? We don't say that everything is good and some things are just less good. In some way we all have some concept of whatever we call right and wrong.

To some extent, our perceptions of reality differ to some degree in all ways. Still, the reality we perceive is one and the same. Fortunately, there is a usual (normal, if you will) range of variation to the differences. Without such we'd have a lot of difficulty with even basic communication.

We perceive reality, at least primarily, through what we call our senses. In one sense, none of us are in direct contact with reality, per se. This is true of all living things. For us homo sapiens, this is referred to as human information processing. For example, light hits our eyes. It is focused on our retinas which contain groups of cells that respond to different information such as color. This is sent to the brain (mostly to parts specialized in analyzing the data) which, with other parts of the brain, finally interprets it and decides what if anything to do with it. In similar ways we perceive reality through all our senses.

Does the color *red* exist? Simply put, I'd say that if the color red doesn't exist then a lot of stuff doesn't exist. We have a red car. Reading that, did you see in your mind's eye a green or yellow or blue car? Of course not. You pictured a red car. There's a good chance you didn't picture the specific model or exact color of red. We refer to a certain spectrum of light as red. That spectrum would include metallic red, fire engine red, blood red, etc. By the same token, you didn't picture a bus or a truck, right?

I believe that there is reality and by virtue of how we are put together and function we perceive that reality. And, despite variances, we perceive it remarkably similarly. Granted, some people are color blind (I am a little bit), some are blind, some deaf, and some have no sense of touch or temperature. These individuals lack or differ in their sense of perception compared to normal (or usual) perception of the same reality.

What if you're a butterfly and I'm dreaming that you're a human? It is important that there is reality and that we all perceive it in basically the same way. A man perceives that he can fly. That is his reality. He perches himself on top a building and readies to take flight. Do you think he will fly? If not, why not? It is his reality. If reality is really relative and individual, then shouldn't we expect him to fly? I think you don't expect him to fly. Just because. Because you know of a thing called gravity, by means of both science and experience, and you know the gravitas of the situation. Perhaps the man has some kind of malfunctioning of usual information processing, biological or psychological. You believe in the law of gravity and you believe that to ignore that law is some kind of malfunction in perception of reality.

I imagine that most of you reading this believe in reality. It is important to me that there is an objective, very consistent and perceptible reality. There are some who believe that there is no reality or that what we call reality is subjective. Objectivity, consistency, and perceptibility in reality is necessary for science and our everyday lives.

A good example of this is the principle of object permanence. Think of a chair. If you have a chair, you expect it to continue to be a chair tomorrow and maybe for several years depending on the condition of the chair. No chair will be a chair forever. But for a reasonable period of time, you expect the chair to not only be a chair but to also be basically the same chair. If the chair is by the table, you expect it to remain by the table. Barring earthquakes, tornadoes, hurricanes, etc. If you are sitting in the chair and stand up, you might sit back down without looking to see if the chair is still there. Without thinking about it, you are demonstrating that you believe in the reality of many things including matter, the chair, gravity, and other physical laws.

Some people think that there is no matter. It is a product of our imagination. They believe we are all spirit and what we think is matter is a product of the spirit. This is difficult for me to understand. Does it matter if there is no matter but you live your life as if there is matter and that matters? Some believe that we are all god. Or, that god is everything and everything is god. I can't speak for you, but I don't feel like I'm god or 7 of 9 of a group consciousness that comprises god. Seems to me that any of these ways of thinking can only end up in some kind of fatalistic and deterministic nihilism; basically, meaning that nothing matters anyway.

Everything I say in the remaining pages has been given serious study and thought by scientists, philosophers, and theologians over many centuries. Regarding anything I say, there are tons of literature supportive and critical of it. I am only a poor student of many great minds. I have enjoyed and somewhat still do, reading in the areas about how do we know what we know (epistemology), the structure of experience and consciousness (phenomenology), and the nature of being and the world that encompasses it (metaphysics, including ontology). I sometimes forget those big words or what they refer to.

My intent here is to share my reasons for believing in God. Some of it comes from my limited understanding of the areas of study mentioned above. My goal is to provide enough food for thought that the reader will consider belief in God a plausible, reasonable choice.

I BELIEVE IN SANTA CLAUS (AND WHAT DOES THAT MEAN?)

Some years before I was a teenager, I was visiting with my twin cousins. They had two ropes tied up between two trees in their yard. The bottom one was a tight rope. Walk on it while hanging on to the other. My cousins were a bit older than me. On my turn, I was scared. My legs began shaking so much that I feared falling off the rope. I believed I could do it, and with much trepidation, I did.

Shortly after, as we talked, I noticed a couple of bicycles and parts next to their garage. I said, "I'm going to ask Santa Claus to give me a bike." My cousins started laughing. They ridiculed me by asking, "You still believe in Santa Claus?" I said, "Yes," which only made it worse for me. More laughter and telling me how dumb I was. There is no Santa Claus!

Well, my parents always told me about Santa Claus. I got gifts from Santa Claus. How could there not be a Santa Claus? Later, at home with my parents I shared this and asked about Santa Claus. To the best of their ability, they tried to explain the whole thing to me. I was really hurt.

I was angry at my parents. How could they let me believe this thing that isn't true? I cried. I didn't put it this way then, but it was like they betrayed my trust. At the age I was, it affected my feelings of trust and perception of reality. It was a major life event for me as silly as that may sound.

And now I'm in my early 70's and I still believe in Santa Claus. It has to do with what is meant by "believe." I came to realize that my parents meant no harm. They wanted me to be part of commonly practiced tradition. They had fun with it and enjoyed my happiness to receive something from Santa.

So, why do I still believe and what does that mean? Well, I don't believe in a jolly man who somehow delivers gifts. I believe that it is a tradition, based on legend and maybe some fact. I enjoyed practicing the tradition with my children. It was still fun, even with my explanation that it was only a tradition.

Let me be clear, the way in which I say I believe in Santa Clause and in God are quite different. It is mostly a matter of semantics and the many ways we use the word "believe."

What does it mean to believe something or believe in something anyway? This is about belief in God. We ask, do you believe in ghosts or extraterrestrial beings or God? We don't ask if you believe in cars or houses. There are many songs that ask things like "do you believe in miracles?" and "do you believe in love?"

Regardless, it is worth a brief look in to what we might mean by "believe." The following definitions are from Dictionary.com.

"Believe" when used as a verb with an object means to have confidence in the truth, the existence, or the reliability of something, although without absolute proof that one is right in doing so. When it is used as a verb, as in, "believe in," it means to be persuaded of the truth or existence of something or to have faith in the reliability, honesty, benevolence, etc. of something.

In the same sense that fairies are imaginary beings and unicorns are mythical animals, I also believe in Santa Claus. What then do I mean when I say I believe in God?

Let's start with what I mean by "God." What, or who, is God? The following definitions are paraphrased from the Concise Oxford American Dictionary.

God (in Christianity and other monotheistic religions) is the creator and ruler of the universe and source of all moral authority; the supreme being. And god (in certain other religions) is a superhuman being or spirit worshipped as having power over nature or human fortunes; a deity.

The dictionary can't cover everything, especially if it's trying to be concise. There are many other ways that people conceptualize what may be referred to as God. These include: God is everything; everything is God; God is in everything; we are God; we are God becoming God; God is the cosmic consciousness; God is G.O.D. (the Guiding, Organizing, Designing principle); and who knows what else.

It is important to me that you have some idea as to why I believe in God in the Judeo-Christian and traditional Christian theological sense. Some of my reasons for belief are basically what I know of current science and some from my understanding of philosophy and theology. All of these interact in different ways and in my world view. The basics of science are hypotheses, experiment, and (possible) replication-- all in the context of research design, methodology, etc. Philosophy is the study of knowledge. What do we know and how do we know it? Heavily reliant on various approaches to logic. Theology is in one sense a philosophical specialty, being the study of God. Although it's often a study of other "studies." Regardless, my beliefs about God include what are called attributes that are stated or derived from statements in the Old and New Testament. For example, God is outside of and in time, at the same time. I will refer to these things as I think they support my belief throughout the rest of my sharing.

Here's a little example. The brilliant Stephen Hawking made a statement that because the big bang was like instantaneous and there was no time until then, God would not have had any time to create anything. But, if you accept the assumption that God is outside of time, and in time, and the creator of time as we know it, then He had all the time in the world, so to speak, to do whatever.

My concept of time interacts with my beliefs in a number of ways. I will discuss that as it applies. In brief, I believe that God is timeless; being the creator of time – time as we know it and any other time that He created. This is a bit theological, and not completely consistent with other thoughts on time that I know of. Biblically, God identified Himself as "I am" and "I am that I am." We lack the capability to comprehend anything that just is. What does that even mean? Honestly, I sure as heck don't know. It makes no sense to me. However, neither do other explanations of our existence to me, as discussed later.

This may be more philosophical than theological, but I've become more of the thought that God exists in "God time." Maybe the use of "time" there isn't right. Our time, which is all we know, was the result of the big bang. It is one dimension of 4 (height, width, depth, time) or up to at least 7 to accommodate string theory, and perhaps up to 11 to 21, depending. In my way of thinking, nothing we could know of (except from external to our time) can be or happen outside of our time. This is how I best understand God and time. He is outside of time as we know it, as time is in our universe. But since God was and did things before the creation of our time, He existed in His time. But there's a lot we don't know. I think maybe there are more, or different, dimensions of time than we know.

In my view of the world, God is spirit. As spirit, He is not matter (unless He wants to take that form; since He created matter anyway). Spirit is outside or beyond how things are and work in the world in which we live. In our world, some consistency of matter and rules of how matter works are necessary for all of science. We have no idea of how to even conceive of being timeless. We are limited by the reality we experience and say we know. We can't put God in a box and study Him. Most of our descriptions are anthropomorphic. That's all we can do. We are in His hands and He sees all and etc. God doesn't have hands or eyes. To say such is a way to express how He is or what He does. Although, God can take on human form with real hands and eyes.

And so, I believe in God (without absolute proof). We all believe in a lot of things without absolute proof! We believe or have faith. The two terms are typically used interchangeably. However, there may be subtle nuanced differences depending on what we are talking about. It makes as much sense to me to believe in God as it does not to believe. The evidence, as I know and understand it, is to me more in favor of belief than not. Beyond that, there is faith. That's slightly different. I admit, in my belief, I am taking a leap of faith. But I believe it is not a blind leap of faith. It is not based on absolute proof, but reasonable with supportive evidence. Yes, I have my doubts and questions. No matter what one believes, they have some. Like Mother Teresa and Billy Graham. Bottom line is that I want you to see why I believe it makes at least as much sense to believe in God as it does not to. My reasons for thinking so I share with you.

EITHER MATTER OR GOD HAS ALWAYS EXISTED

It may sound silly, but an age-old philosophical question is "Why is there something at all instead of nothing?" People have pondered this and written many volumes discussing it. Of course, if there was nothing, no one would ask why is there nothing. I accept the existence and reality of something. The question for me is where did matter come from.

The way I see it is that there are only three suggested answers to this question. The first is that matter has always existed. The second is that something comes from nothing. The third is that God has always existed and created matter.

In the past it seemed as sensible to believe that the universe had always existed as it did to believe that the earth is flat and the center of the universe. It is now generally accepted that the universe has not always existed. It is the result of what we call the big bang. This has to do with the creation of the universe and not the creation of matter, per se. The idea is that there was a point of singularity or something infinitesimally small that somehow went bang and over many billions of years ended up producing the universe and all that's in it. A basic decision or choice that I must make is about whether matter has always existed or that God has always existed and is the creator of matter. I still think those are my choices despite the Big Bang, explanations of something coming from nothing, and thoughts about how matter doesn't exist. However small, and however many (multi-verses), or bouncing universes, it was still something. Whatever it be, it either always existed or was created.

I believe that I and matter exist. My body is matter. If I fall down the stairs and break my neck by hitting other matter [did that], that matters! There are some who would say that such is just an illusion or such. They'd say that in some way each of us is the divine mind or cosmic consciousness or part of it, seeing ourselves or becoming ourselves – God seeing God or God becoming God

This line of thought is contained in some Eastern religions and philosophies. You may be aware of this way of thinking as presented in Christian Science. In this view of everything, matter does not exist— all is spiritual. God (a Principle with no personhood or personality) is all that exists and what we perceive as matter is an interpretation of divine mind. [from *Science and Health with Key to the Scriptures*, by Mary Baker Eddy, 1866]

Criticism of this, and other similar points of view, are made scientifically, philosophically, and theologically. Indulge me for a moment to share a related, somewhat tangential story. I was blessed to take some graduate level classes under Dr. James Strauss. He used to say that Christian Science was neither Christian nor science. This has nothing to do with the veracity of his statement, but I share this because of its effect on me. Dr. Strauss was an awesome dude. I mean, he studied at Tubingen and many prestigious places, but chose to teach at a humble little college in Lincoln, Illinois. On a couple of occasions, I saw him loan a graduate student a stack of three to five books and ask for their return the next day! He was one of those people that could read a page just like that. There was a thing going around that he read books while mowing his lawn. I doubted that. Then I saw it. No kidding, he was pushing the mower and reading. And, he ate in the cafeteria with us students. There was a saying about the college: it was a good place to train missionaries because there was hot and cold, and if you can eat the cafeteria food you could eat anything. In terms of the food, whether we liked it or not, it was something.

So, where did the matter, the unimaginably, infinitesimally small something come from? The easiest thing for me to think is that it just always existed. For a lot of scientific reasons including the math and all, this line of thought isn't adequate for many in the scientific community. Partly because of the intriguing study of quantum mechanics and physics, there is a thought that something came from nothing. It's been suggested that it is the nature of nothing to become something. Please note that if nothing has a nature, it's not nothing. And, as strange as it sounds it would also mean that nothing always existed. This gets a bit bizarre to me as it seems more philosophical than scientific. I'm referring to what is meant by the word "nothing."

In common parlance, if we open a box and don't see a thing, we say there's nothing in there. Others know what we mean. There's nothing we perceive or care about. We don't mean that there is something we might call nothing in there. We don't mean that the box is devoid of air, dust, microorganisms, gravity, radiation, quantum particles, negative energy, or anything, or everything. Just the same as what we call empty space isn't empty at all.

In his book *The Wonder of the World*, Varghese discusses eight ontological (the branch of metaphysics dealing with the nature of being) principles that he utilizes to basically support the existence of God. His third principle addresses the idea of something from nothing. His summary of this discussion is a better presentation of my line of thought and more succinct. The following is part of his summary. "Over the centuries thinkers who have considered the concept of nothing have been careful to emphasize the point that nothing is not a kind of something. Absolute nothingness can never be the object of scientific inquiry because all such inquiry presupposes the existence of the object of study and of some order governing the behavior of the object. … The nothing that contemporary cosmologists and quantum physicists discuss always turns out to be something in disguise." (Varghese 2003, 132-133)

I think that I'm old enough to have thought that the universe was static, even if created by God. I now accept that the universe is not static, but still believe it was created by God.

This is a basic consideration for me. Well, if something that mattered has always existed, then God didn't create it. In and of itself, that would challenge my Christian world view.

It was suggested to me once that maybe matter and God have both always existed forever. My first thought was that's crazy. After reflecting on it, I guess that such might be hypothetically possible. That is the only time I've heard that idea. Historically, it is easy to understand why this would not be considered a viable theory by either atheists or theists. Since it was believed that matter and the universe had always existed, there was no need to consider a god that was beyond our scientific inquiry. That being now questioned, atheists propose the above-mentioned ideas that something comes from nothing. It must if there is no God. In general, theists believe that God has always existed and created all we know -- matter and the universe. There is no compelling reason for trying to juxtapose these two world views.

I believe in matter. Since most of my life involves matter, it is easy to believe in matter. It makes up a lot of all that matters to us, right?

EVIDENCE OF DESIGN IN CREATION AND LIFE

The basic idea behind this line of thought is that if somethings appears to have been designed, then there's likely a designer. This is commonly referred to as the watchmaker argument. It goes something like the following.

If you were a person who had never seen a watch and came across one while walking on the beach, you'd find it interesting. If you figured out that it tells time, you'd likely think that it was made to do so. Someone designed the thing. And, beyond that, it was designed with the purpose of telling time. Take this line of reasoning and apply it to the universe. The universe is very complex and works. Likewise, people are very complex and work. You may think that all these things were designed and for some purpose. This makes sense to me.

However, maybe everything is just the result of random things happening. Things do happen randomly or so it seems. Not so much so things that function and serve a purpose. I'm in awe over the number of things that all have to work and continue to work in order for the universe to exist. Let alone, a universe that is suitable for us to live in.

One aspect of design implies order. Order that is imposed upon process, either by an external, autonomous and necessarily intelligent agent or by a law (and from whence the law?). True randomness, or what we would call pure randomness, does not produce order. It produces either chaos or homogeneity. Such homogeneity we could say is orderly, but it is of little or no use.

Without something intervening, the second law of thermodynamics says that things deconstruct or fall apart (lose order). There are many examples in life that illustrate this point. Granted, some of these things seem either self-evident or stupid to ponder. Yet, they are interesting because it seems more intuitively and experientially reasonable that things are prone to break down or fall apart rather than to produce order, especially the complex order that is necessary for the existence of the universe and life.

Remember the watch maker? If you took a watch apart and threw the pieces in the air or stirred them in a pot for billions of times or years, do you think a watch would appear? Or, would you expect to come across a beautiful sand painting on the beach, without assuming that someone created it? And then, it would have to be sustained or by wind, rain, or waves it will be gone. If you take some shirts out of the dryer or already folded ones and toss them up, do you expect them to land folded? Even if you did it for billions of years? If you take all the letters of the alphabet many times over and throw them up, a word may fall out. If you throw them up again, that word will likely not be there, and you need several words to make a multi-word sentence. What are the odds of getting a multi-word sentence on one throw? In an evolutionary sense, something must keep the one word together to mix with another word and then another to end up with a multi-word sentence.

The point here is that randomness does not produce order. The amount of order and laws (which may be orderly or produce order) that are required for the universe and life is way beyond my comprehension. The following discussion presents just a few that are truly amazing to me and to me are signs that point to an autonomous and intelligent creator of laws and order.

I believe that things change over time (evolve). But the theory of evolution is still a theory even though there is a lot of belief in it. I have limited understanding of serious biological arguments in this regard. I may be wrong, but I doubt the primordial pool as the source of my own being. A theory that depends on survival of the fittest, assumes the arrival of the fittest. There may be some randomness involved. It is getting harder to treat bacteria. Are we evolving to beat them?

However, randomness isn't exactly random. There is an underlying order to randomness. A major part of my educational background is social psychology. I am familiar with survey methodology and the bell-shaped curve that underlies our approach to many things. So, when I first encountered this thought I was stumped. I mean, if you are doing a survey, you want to draw a random sample. In this sense, any order would imply that you don't have a random sample. When I got a better grasp on this, I was relieved to know that this wasn't directly related to what I was concerned about.

Basically, it is about the order that is inherent in randomness, as in how randomness produces the bell-shaped curve. My introduction to the bell-shaped curve came by way of being graded on the curve. It is a rather crude way to assign a value to someone's performance on one test for many reasons. Regardless, there is an average (mean) score of all test takers. That would be the top of the curve. Mathematically, other scores can be calculated as being one or two standard deviations above or below and used to assign a grade. Another way you may know about the idea of the bell-shaped curve has to do with IQ tests. Here's a mathematical example. If you randomly pick a number from 1 to 100 one hundred times and calculate the average of those numbers and repeat this process one hundred times and plot the averages, you will end up with something close to a near-perfect bell-shaped curve.

The idea here is that random sampling of numbers produces a predictable bell-shaped curve. Why should such be the case? There appears to be some order to randomness for some reason, or because of some reason. In concluding a chapter on this subject, Schwartz says the following. "Order does not occur by chance – but neither does randomness. The logic becomes inexorable. The conclusion becomes inescapable. If complex orders do not occur by chance … and we discover replicable evidence of complex order (be they in sand paintings or in sequences of numbers we experience as melodies and harmonies), then we can't logically draw the conclusion that the replicated orders could have occurred by chance alone. *Chance per se is no longer a plausible explanation for the existence of order.* It's that simple." (Schwartz 2006, 53)

Hate to admit it, but I'm not smart enough to make good use of my smart phone. I believe that someone designed it to do things that I don't comprehend. Just because I can't comprehend it, doesn't mean I don't believe it. It's a technological invention that remarkably works and I pay to use it. I've no idea what 5G might mean. Hopefully not more confusion for me.

Closer to home, to the best of my understanding, we need helpful bacteria to live. Bacteria that is somewhat but not necessarily symbiotic or parasitic. And, everyone has or has had cancer or pre-cancerous cells but our body tends to take care of it. At so many levels and in so many ways, everything is complex and complicated. I'm amazed that anything works let alone all of it together.

Because of more recent advances and discoveries, thanks to astronomy, cosmology, and astrophysics, it is generally accepted that the universe as we know it is not eternal. The universe we know started with an event that is referred to as the big bang. The research (which in and of itself is very complex and complicated and mostly beyond this simple man) indicates that the age of the universe is 13.82 billion years (plus or minus 20 million years). The age of our galaxy, the Milky Way, is 11 to 13 billion years. And, the age of our planet Earth is about 4.54 billion years. Yes, in some ways time is relative but that's how it is in the way we measure time. I don't tend to think about things with that many numbers. Like if I lived to be 100, I'd have to live ten million life times to be a billion years old. Or, if I was counting dollar bills at the rate of one per second non-stop, it would take me 31.69 years to hit one billion. There's a lot of time involved with these things. Yet, note that the times are not infinite and not even trillions or quadrillions of years.

From all I can tell, the general scientific consensus is that ever since the big bang the universe has been expanding. It was very, very fast at first. Then a bit slower for reasons beyond me. And since then, continuing to expand at a faster rate. Honestly, there are some detractors to this view.

Regardless, this is interesting to me. Can the universe continue to exist and expand forever? Most astrophysicists say no. Either way, the outcome will be that our universe will cease to exist. This is not an existential threat. The estimates for this that I've read are one to three trillion years. That doesn't really matter. Our sun will die, burn out, in about 5.5 billion years from now. If by then we can get to a habitable planet, then we could live until that sun dies, etc. But only up until the time that the universe ceases to exist. It may then collapse to an infinitesimal singularity and have to become a universe again. So, say some. However, the use of the word "time" in regard to that is awkward if you believe that the space time continuum was created via the big bang.

Since scientific consensus, for the most part, held that the universe always existed or did so for many billions of years, it was thought there was plenty time for the right things to just happen to come together and eventually produce life. Some of these assumptions have become more questionable and complicated.

One complication is the big bang itself. Based on studies of background radiation with other measurements, many researchers place the age of the universe at 13.8 billion years and the age of the earth around 4.45 billion years. This may seem like a long time. However, there were not an infinite number of rolls of the cosmic dice.

Another complication is the age of the first identifiable life on earth. In his book, *The Hidden Face of God*, Schroeder discusses the work of Elso Barghoorn. In the 1970's, Barghoorn examined rocks that were the oldest that could bear fossils using an electron microscope. He found fossil evidence of fully developed bacteria in 3.6-billion-year-old rocks. With further study, he discovered indications of cellular life around 3.8 billion years ago, around the time that liquid water first appeared on earth. This is scientifically interesting because there is evidence of life on earth much less than one billion years after the universe gave birth to the earth. "Overnight, the fantasy of billions of years of random reactions in warm little ponds brimming with fecund chemicals leading to life, evaporated. Elso Barghoorn had discovered a most perplexing fact: life, the most complexly organized system of atoms known in the universe, popped into being in the blink of a geological eye." (Schroeder 2001, 51-52)

Schroeder shares comments related to these matters by Nobel laureate, organic chemist and a leader in origin of life studies, Christian de Duve, from de Duve's book, *Tour of a Living Cell.* "The speed at which evolution started moving once it discovered the right track, so to speak, and the apparently autocatalytic manner by which it accelerated are truly astonishing …. [Yet] chance and chance alone did it all. But it is not, as some would have it, the whole answer, for chance did not operate in a vacuum. It operated in a universe governed by orderly laws and made of matter endowed with special properties. These laws and properties are the constraints that shape evolutionary roulette and restrict the numbers that can turn up …. Faced with the enormous sum of lucky draws behind the success of the evolutionary game, one may legitimately wonder to what extent this success is actually written into the fabric of the universe." (Schroeder 2001,51-52)

What is life anyway? I thought there would be a straight forward scientific answer. Not necessarily. I found that in general, science says that there are seven life processes. If something contains these seven processes, then it would be considered alive. However, I found two different lists of the seven processes and I can only make out that there are four items that are common to each list. You can check this out, but here are the seven items from each list. In one list the processes are movement, respiration, sensitivity, nutrition, excretion, reproduction, and growth. In another list the processes are response to stimuli, metabolize energy, produce offspring, grow, maintain stable body temperature, consist of one or more cells, and adapt to the environment. Seems that at some level, something is alive depending on your definition of life.

At the time of writing, the COVID-19 infection is still rampant. I was intrigued to hear some folks talk about killing it and others say that you can't kill it because it isn't alive. To me it seems that applying either of the lists of seven processes would indicate that it's not alive. One reason is that it can't reproduce without entering a cell. So, someone says that if you consider life something that can replicate itself with the help of a cell, then you could call it alive. Just a matter of definition.

Regardless, even if there be some gray areas, there is what we call life. I'm of the opinion that life doesn't come from non-life. I don't think that mixing up a lot of chemicals can result in life. So far, science has not been able to create life from non-life. It has been thought that such was done. However, what was produced was the necessary material for life. And, even that has not been replicated that I know of.

In his discussion of life, Varghese states, "Thus, we are led to the conclusion that life of any kind cannot come from non-life. In the ultimate analysis life must spring from a transcendent Source that is not simply living but is Itself Life in all its fullness." He further presents a statement by Dr. Warner Arber, who was a winner of the Nobel prize for discovery of restrictive enzyme. Arber wrote: "1. Life only starts at the level of a functional cell; 2. The most primitive cells require several hundred different specific biological macro-molecules; 3. It is a mystery how such already complex structures came together; and, 4. The possibility of a Creator, of God, represents a satisfactory solution to this problem." (Varghese 2003, 54)

That there is anything at all has been of great interest for the longest time. That there is life is awesome and even of greater interest. Especially life that can have interest and experience awe while also reflecting on the interest and awe.

What if science was able to create life? I'm doubtful, but perhaps it's theoretically possible. If that happened, there are several reasons why it wouldn't detract from my belief in God. Life, in and of itself, is a long way from conscious, intelligent, autonomous agents. Whatever science creates, it creates from things that already exist. Science would be working with matter and with the rules attending matter. Also, it wouldn't be the result of random luck as science is an intervening, intelligent, purposeful force. In efforts to create life, science is essentially seeking to replicate the creation of life.

It seems to me that there are rules or laws involved with everything that is. Some rules apply to the creation of the universe, the continued existence of the universe, and life itself. The rules we know about are universal and maybe all are not implicit or inherent in the things they apply to. This principle permeates many of the reasons I believe.

Simply put, the thing controlled by rules isn't responsible for the rules. The rules or laws had to proceed it. Hence, from whence the rules or laws?

I find it interesting that, in one sense, everything is one thing – energy. But energy is manifested in many forms. Every atom is like a small solar system, wherein electrons orbit the nucleus like planets orbit the sun. There's a lot of space in there at the atomic level and much more at subatomic levels. Molecules are made of atoms. Atoms consist of a nucleus (typically a neutron and proton) and electron(s) along with photons, neutrinos, gluons, muons, quarks, etc., along with the four forces of the strong and weak nuclear forces, electromagnetic forces, and gravity which hold it together and allow it to do what an atom does. If not for these forces, for various reasons, there wouldn't be anything that we perceive as matter. The forces that hold it all together keep us from sliding through the floor, so to speak. If we poke at a piece of wood it seems solid to us. But we can hammer a nail in to the wood. The forces that hold the nail together are stronger than the forces that hold the wood together. And, so what, right? That's just the way it is. Nice that it works for us though. Even though we don't know exactly how, let alone why. In science this might be called a "given" or otherwise identified as a brute fact. Science will continue to research the how part. The why part has to be addressed through scientific philosophy or metaphysical science. Obviously, there are rules involved.

It is also interesting to me that there is order to chaos. Getting my head around this did cause some brain strain. But, after some re-reading of Gleick's book, *CHAOS*, I'm more comfortable. This book was maybe the first attempt to present to us regular folks an introduction to the history of the relatively new theories and science of chaos. The more I processed and pondered the information, the more the basic premises seemed intuitively understandable. As I get it, the science of chaos is basically about discovering the order within what otherwise is considered to be or appears to be chaos.

This is rather complicated stuff and I don't pretend to understand the mathematics or physics behind this area of science. The basic idea is that something that seems chaotic may not be chaotic at all when studied using other tools and methodologies. The important part of this to me has to do with the studies of events that produce results that appear chaotic in and of themselves. However, everything is related, not just at the time of the study but also over time. The science of chaos indicates that the more factors that you add in to the formula and follow it over time, there is order not seen otherwise.

Allow me to share this from Gleick's book. "Chaos has created special techniques of using computers and special kinds of graphic images, pictures that capture a fantastic and delicate structure underlying complexity. ... To some physicists, chaos is a science of process rather than state, of becoming rather than being .... No matter what the medium, the behavior obeys the same newly discovered laws." (Gleick 1987, 4-5)

Notice the reference to laws. My take is simply that we often perceive chaos (or randomness) because we don't see the larger picture. Sort of like not seeing the forest for the trees. And, I think that applies to many things.

There is also much more to design than that which exists in matter and rules and laws of nature. There are our perceptions of things composed of matter at the physical level. And, there are our perceptions of things that are non-material. In finishing this chapter on design, I delve briefly in to some related philosophical and theological matters that support my belief in God. Philosophically, I'm talking about the area of phenomenology which deals with the structures of experience and consciousness, and the meaning things have in our experience. Theologically, I share my understanding of how God is revealed in the design of creation. It seems easier for me to approach this from these two perspectives, but they are similar and interrelated.

When I see a flower, I see a flower. I don't, because I can't, see all of the complex systems of the flower or the molecules and atoms that comprise it. Yet, in one sense, at that level, it is only various atoms. However, it is certain atoms of certain elements in certain amounts and arranged in certain ways to be something we call a flower. As in, a rose by any other name is still a rose. And still, it can be perceived as something more than a rose. If you give a rose or bouquet to someone, it might be perceived as a gift representing *love* – or you might *hope* so. It might be perceived as *beautiful*. So, a flower that is a rose can be so much more.

In one sense, a poem is only letters, though letters arranged to make words and words arranged to make sentences and sentences arranged to give sense to the collection of sentences. And, we understand it via our senses and language with our consciousness, emotion, and intelligence. Similar to a painting, which is in one sense only atoms… etc. But we perceive a painting. It didn't randomly appear. It was painted. We assume that it was painted by a painter. We may or may not *like* the painting, that doesn't matter. The painting we perceive was created with a design in the mind of its creator.

In *The Wonder of the World*, Varghese says that we see God in everything. My understanding of what he means is that if we see the wonder of and behind all these things, we see God. I might state that a bit differently, like: in all these things we see the handiwork of God.

Schroeder, in *The Hidden Face of God*, takes the approach that everything is information. Obviously, any law or rule consists of or at least contains information. For example, when the human sperm and egg meet up, they have all the information to create everything that ends up being a human being. Information does not come from nothing. Inherently, it has to come from something that has information and capability to share, in whatever way, information. Bottom line is that he says, in my understanding, that God is the source of information, being ultimate, transcendent, intelligence. So, when we perceive anything, it is both intelligent and the result of intelligence. Therefore, when we see anything that is a result of intelligence (information) we see God. Again, I say we see the work of God, a slight but maybe significant difference.

C. S. Lewis speaks of things in nature and our experience as pointers or sign posts, like trail markers. In his book, *Surprised by Joy*, he describes having the experience of joy, which became something that he desired. However, he discovered that what he really was seeking was that to which joy pointed – the source of joy: God.

I assume that everyone has at some time had the experience of being overcome with awe, been struck by beauty, awash with wonder, filled with joy. One definition of "glory" is the manifestation of God's presence as perceived by humans. This is expressed in the Bible as follows. "The heavens declare the glory of God, the vault of heaven proclaims his handiwork, day discourses it to day, night to night hands on the knowledge. No utterance at all, no speech, not a sound to be heard, but from the entire earth the design stands out, this message reaches the entire world." (Psalms 19: 1-4)

In concluding this chapter, I say that I believe there is evidence of design (order, rules/laws) in creation and life. The universe and life are very complex. The complexities are given order by rules and laws that govern the nature of all that exists. Randomness doesn't produce order even though there is order in randomness. It seems to me that something never comes from nothing. Likewise, rules or laws didn't come from nothing. Left alone things basically fall apart. Thus, I believe there is a designer, a creator of rules and laws, and something (or someone) that holds it all together, a sustainer, and I believe that is God.

CONSCIOUSNESS, INTELLIGENCE, LANGUAGE, AND FREE WILL

I t seems appropriate to me to discuss these topics together. I mean, you have to be conscious and have a sense of consciousness to discuss consciousness, right? To discuss consciousness, you have to have some kind of intelligence, ability to think and comprehend. To have a discussion you have to communicate, much of which we do is typically via language. I admit that my reasons for including free will here may be a bit tenuous. However, at some level it seems to me that one could not have free will if one had no consciousness, intelligence, or way to analyze choices. Notwithstanding that some thought processes may be experiential or emotional or visual.

There's a little ditty I've seen in several places which I'd like you to keep in mind as you read the rest of this chapter. It goes as follows. A student asks the professor, "How do I know I exist?" The professor responds, "Who's asking?"

Language is perhaps the easiest of these topics to discuss, but let's start with consciousness. Everyone I've met seems to believe that they have consciousness, except for in a different way when they are unconscious. As in, to some extent we are unconscious while sleeping. Yet, not completely and to different degrees at different times. Sleeping and dreaming are very interesting to me. If you've traveled a lot, you've probably woken up some time and for a second wondered where you were. Regardless, you know that you are still you.

Consciousness is a complicated subject. You have to be conscious to know that you're conscious – at least at some level. It's been an object of interest to scientists and philosophers since either existed. What is consciousness anyway? The dictionary says: "the state of being awake and aware of one's surroundings, the awareness or perception of something by a person, the fact of awareness by the mind of itself and the world." Interesting that the definition introduces the concept of *mind*. And, how does the dictionary define mind: "the element of a person that enables them to be aware of the world and their experiences, to think, and to feel; the faculty of consciousness and thought…." Quite straightforward, yes?

Scientifically, especially medically, you are unconscious if you are knocked out or anesthetized or such. Some matters of degree. If you are just sleeping and someone starts to cut through your chest to perform heart surgery, I bet you're usually fully conscious really quick. If you are anesthetized you are not aware of all the sawing and cutting going on. Been there, through that. But you are quite aware afterwards! And yet, you are still the same person with the same consciousness.

Someone might ask about amnesia, brain damage, and things like Alzheimer's. It is sad to hear someone say that their spouse is not there anymore. These are things affecting normal function. Sometimes a person may not recognize you, but they will tell you stories about their life. For a moment they might show they know who you are. Just because you can't remember who you are doesn't mean that you aren't the same person. To a large extent these are exceptions to the rule, anomalies. Interesting that amnesia can result from psychological trauma. That has to involve some kind of mind brain connection. In these circumstances, whether the person can communicate it or not, I believe they exist with the same consciousness. One example would be how someone may be in a comma for many years and then come to as their same old self.

That's about all that science can do with consciousness. You are conscious, semi-conscious, or unconscious. Notwithstanding altered states of consciousness and the study thereof. Like mind-altering drugs, psychotropics, sensory deprivation, meditation, etc. Whatever, it is still a study of the effects of something on something called consciousness, not a direct study of consciousness.

From what I understand, when people speak of the mind they are speaking more of actions of the brain. Consciousness is more so thought of as something that is related to, interdependent, and interrelated with the brain. Over thousands of years there's been many philosophical attempts to address what the heck it is that comprises consciousness. It's some strange and boring stuff, but check out some items in the bibliography for starters if that's your thing. Historically, much of the writings in this area are about the soul. Different ways to discuss what is it that is you when you say "I" or refer to yourself as "me".

I believe I have consciousness. There is an I that is me. Even though the cells of my body change many times, I am still me. How is this so?

Where I'm going with that is simple -- matter, per se, does not produce or contain consciousness. You might philosophically or religiously disagree on this, but I don't think that a rock knows (is conscious) it's a rock and contemplates how that is or what it means. There was either always matter that evolved in to life that is conscious or always a God of ultimate consciousness who created everything, and imparted consciousness.

Some will say that as we evolved our brains ended up creating our consciousness. Or something like that. Ok, but I just don't see it. It is one thing to me that requires an outside of time/space consciousness to impart. I just be stating my opinion, the way I see things.

People have pursued immortality forever, so to speak. Like the fountain of youth and such. Some people who believe that our consciousness and who we are is a result of electro-biochemical processes, think that we might be able to have that digitalized, and hence live forever in a sense. I doubt that. But, even if possible, it has nothing to do with whether or not that it was God who ultimately made it possible. I can't imagine it to be anything that interests me personally. Besides, one might "live" longer, but that life will still come to an end sometime in some way.

On to thoughts about intelligence. We tend to think about how smart you are; how much do you know, in general. Or, is your IQ 100 or above 130? As I've aged, I think mine has dropped; however, my background included administering the Weschler and Stanford-Binet. I found it quite intriguing. But there is whatever intelligence is and there are street smarts and there is common sense. And you know they ain't all the same! I worked with a guy who was a MENSA member. Many years ago, he committed what we'd probably consider a significant cyber financial crime. From what he said, he turned himself in basically thinking that would be better for him than being caught. Maybe that was smart. He was plenty intelligent, but how smart was it to do the crime when he could've made plenty without doing the crime?

I'll go back to my talk about the rock. Generally speaking, I say the rock can't talk. In some sense, perhaps a rock has its own story. That's partly in what you mean. My Native American heritage tells me that all things are of the Great Spirit and He may speak to us through any of His creation. That's beyond my understanding. Regardless, if a rock has any intelligence (and I'm sure it does in the sense of information, like everything), it came from outside of the rock itself.

Speaking of a rock, it may speak to us in different ways. In terms of language, such is actually an amazing thing. There are many forms of communication or sharing information that happens between animals and plants. However, linguists like Noam Chomsky have said that language is innate to humans. Our human language communication is qualitatively different. This used to be widely accepted among linguists and philosophers. However, this is another thing that depends largely upon how you define it.

Things "communicate." Trees being eaten by giraffes give off a scent that alerts other trees to put in their leaves something giraffes don't like to protect themselves. This is communication, the sharing of information. But is it language? They don't discuss the weather, how was your day, or what is the meaning of life. Does a plant feel pain? My Native ancestors (and some others) say so. Got a bit off track there.

Language may not be limited to humans. It may be qualitatively different for humans but also as much so quantitatively. Deaf people signing was not considered language by many for a long time. Mostly because it didn't involve talking. It has since been accepted as language. Well, it has to be a language to translate convoluted political speech or scientific presentations.

The experiments and research involving ASL with chimpanzees may indicate that chimps can talk via ASL. Their vocal apparatus doesn't allow for making human sounds. I say "may" because that is debated. The same is true for young children. The chimps can evidently communicate with the vocabulary of a 2- to 3-year-old child. As a father, I thought I was talking, even at an infantile level, with my three-year-old's.

My point is that language is a unique thing. Seems obvious to be interrelated with intelligence. Also seems, except for the visual imaging, some ESP, or such, necessary to receive or transmit thoughts or ideas, etc. As such, I consider language something that requires an outside entity that created language or at least the propensity for language.

And now to the seemingly easy one, free will. I say seemingly easy because everyone I know acts as if they have free will; yet some will be deterministic or fatalistic in their thoughts. To be strictly materialistic, you probably have to believe that everything about you has been or is being determined by your genes, your experience, and your circumstances.

I say that people act as if they have free will for a lot of reasons. If you get your spouse an anniversary gift, you like to think that you chose to do so. And you like to think that your spouse believes that you did so because you chose to. I know, it sounds silly. You don't think that you did so because it just was that you had to and you don't want your spouse to think that you only did it because you had no choice. Perhaps you forgot your anniversary. It's not your fault. It was predetermined that you would. Is the spouse going to feel that way?

Granted, some time we have no choice. That's the exception rather than the rule. When I was thirteen my grandma stayed with us. One time when only the two of us were home, she kept walking around the house and asking where the baby was. I was freaked out as there was no baby. Obviously, she had some kind of dementia. The misfiring, malfunctioning synoptic connections and such created in her mind that she should find the baby. Because of that she chose to look for the baby. Well, if that is your experience, who wouldn't look for the baby? My take on that is that such is not fatalistic determinism. She made a rational choice given the information she had.

Similar, but different, is someone who is innocent by means of insanity. Say someone kills someone because they believe that God told them to do it. If they really believe that, the choice to do it is not completely irrational. To delve further in to these kinds of things would require discussion of medical and legal ethics.

Those kinds of things are not the norm. The brain decision making process, intimate with consciousness, has been interfered with. It's a sad thing and considered abnormal, hence all the research in these areas.

As **I** write this and **you** read it, can you deny that **we** are conscious? The bottom line for me is that material things aren't conscious and there's no evidence that they become conscious.

In terms of free will, I believe I chose to write this. I think you chose to read this. The concept has been given a whole lot of attention in philosophy and theology. There's still no complete agreement about the basics in both or between both fields of thought.

MORALITY AND EMOTIONS

When I was a young boy, my dad would say to me, with a chuckle, "You're a good boy. Just don't know what you're good for." As a parent, I had my idea of when my children were being good. That implies that I also had my idea of when they were being bad. The subject here relates to the concept of good and bad, or right and wrong – not what is right or wrong. And, also emotions related to feeling good or bad, or happy or sad.

Although a culture or an individual may have different ideas about what is right and wrong, they have some concept of right and wrong. Their concept of right or wrong may be right or wrong, but there is the concept. There may be a culture in which a child may be sacrificed to a god. It may be considered the right thing to do. Some would say that such proves that all is morally relative. I might say that the mores of that culture are wrong. It's as possible for a culture to be wrong as it is for any person to be wrong. Right?

This is an area like all areas of thought in which there has been serious study and writing for centuries. I only share my thoughts based on the best of my understanding and how it relates to why I am a theist.

The basic consideration here has to do with how is it that people have a sense of right and wrong at all. How is that? Even if consciousness is just a result of bioelectric physical functioning, that wouldn't imply that the concept of morality is a result of the same functioning or a creation of consciousness. Morality is not a necessary component or product of consciousness. As discussed earlier, there are differing ideas about what consciousness is. And, it cannot be studied directly. This not about what is right or wrong, it is about how does the concept of right and wrong exist.

I don't believe that consciousness came from innate matter. I similarly do not believe that the universal concept of morality came from innate matter. A rock is not alive. A rock is not conscious. A rock has no sense of morality. It is my contention that a rock, per se, will never come alive, become conscious, or have any sense of morality.

Consider a straight line and a crooked line. If you had only ever seen straight lines, you wouldn't have a concept of a crooked line. But when you see a crooked line, you know it is not a straight line. Technically, there may not be a true straight line in our existence. It may be a hypothetical construct that works for purposes of physics and such. I'm using it as an analogy, as have others. There is no material reason for us to have a concept of right and wrong. Things just are. Yet, we have the concept of right and wrong.

My take is that any concept of morality did not evolve from matter. It therefore came from an autonomous, moral entity. I know, you might disagree. Just saying it the way I see it.

Emotions are different but related to morality. Unless we're approaching emotions from a philosophical point of view, we basically don't have a concept of emotions; we experience emotions. We experience love, hate, happiness and sadness. The same kind of question asked regarding morality applies to emotions. How is it that emotions exist?

When talking about emotions, I assume that we have a similar idea as to what is meant. On the other hand, we don't much think about what is an emotion anyway. My dictionary describes emotion as follows: a natural instinctive state of mind deriving from one's circumstances, mood, or relationships with others; any of the particular feelings that characterize such a state of mind, such as joy, anger, love, hate, horror, etc.; instinctive or intuitive feeling as distinguished from reasoning or knowledge. Somehow, we know what it is but it's not that easy to describe.

Emotions are very interesting. For one thing, they are personal. You and I could look out the same window and see the same rain falling. You might feel happy about it. I might feel sad and disappointed. So, obviously it is not the rain that causes a particular emotional reaction.

Emotions are interesting in being something that we experience vicariously. You watch a film. Someone is severely snubbed by one they love. You know that feeling. You feel sad for them. It is only a movie. It isn't real. Yet, your feeling is real and you may even cry real tears.

Ever see a guy watching a baseball game where a guy catches a ball in his crotch? The guy watching acts like he's in pain. Nothing happened to him. He is empathizing with the guy who is obviously in pain.

Furthermore, you have probably experienced an emotion as if it was physical pain. If your child gets injured, you hurt with them. If you've lost a child, you hurt. I sympathize. Mine was 21, but still my child. I hurt. Ain't nobody going to tell you that's not real.

I don't believe that consciousness is some epiphenomenon arising from matter. I mean only from matter without any external guidance. I don't believe that any concept of morality or emotions came from matter without any external influence. I don't think that a rock is conscious and thus it doesn't contemplate why it is a rock. A rock has no sense of right and wrong and doesn't feel good or bad about anything. At least as far as I know.

In these regards, it seems to me that an external, autonomous, intelligent, conscious, entity is necessary for the nonmaterial, metaphysical things like consciousness, intelligence, the concept of morality and emotions to exist. I believe that entity is God.

There is a principle in philosophy which states that to build a thing, you need the proper materials. Simply put, this is the same as saying you need lumber to build a log cabin and you cannot build a log cabin with bricks. Some apply this to the metaphysical things mentioned above. For example, you can't build an emotion out of a rock. It is almost by definition; you can't build something metaphysical out of the physical. God, by definition, is immaterial. He is spirit. Thus, He is the source of these metaphysical things within the physical universe.

ARGUMENTS AGAINST GOD

This also can be complicated and convoluted. I'm a simple man and it seems to me that most of the arguments against God are basically the antithesis of arguments for God. In one sense, since the existence of God cannot be proven or disproven, you believe one way or the other based on your understanding of the evidence (scientifically, philosophically, historically and experientially). Regardless, you believe one way or the other. Your choice is ultimately mostly a matter of faith – you choose, for whatever reasons, to believe one thing or another. My point in writing this is to share why I believe and make the statement that it makes (at least) as much sense (scientifically, philosophically, historically and experientially) to be a theist as to be an atheist.

For sake of discussion, I divide the arguments against God as being either scientific or philosophical and personal.

The scientific arguments are primarily that God is not necessary because: 1.) either matter has always existed or comes from nothing; 2.) evolution does not require God for what is, for life or humanity; and, 3.) there is no evidence of God scientifically. The philosophical and personal objections to believe in God seem to boil down to: 1.) belief in God or anything "supernatural" is harmful to humankind, is delusional or a psychiatric problem, as in religion ruins everything and is therefore "evil" (evidently a problem that evolution has yet to remedy?), or 2.) how could there be a God when there is so much pain and suffering -- let alone the how could or why did this happen to me question.

I've already commented about the matter or matter from nothing issues. Current Christian writers differ in details about evolution. It may sound simplistic, but I believe God created all that is including us. And, being not all that smart, it doesn't matter to me if He initiated a process that came to fulfillment or actively interacted in the process. Phenomenologically, I perceive (am consciously aware of) being here, being me, and although I may sometime act as dumb as a rock, I don't think I'm a rock. Maybe you can relate to that in some way.

This next part has to be a bit philosophical and theological. I am not a good student of history. I am enough so to acknowledge that atrocious things have been and are done in the name of some religion. But my little knowledge also tells me that much good has been done in the name of some religion. People can do good and bad. If you're like me, I gather you have done both.

I think that the following thoughts fit here. Consider the following philosophically and logically, if a being or entity is required – for life, consciousness, emotion, intelligence, etc. -- it is not required to meet our ideas of what it should be. God is who He is. First, who are we to question him? Then, there is the issue of free will. From whence, what we call evil?

Regarding the first issue, some say they can't believe in a God who allows such pain and suffering. The first question is whether or not there is a God. Not whether if there is a God that God is who you want that God to be. If there is a God, then you can seek to know about who that God is. Whether or not there is a God, or the necessity for an autonomous, external, intelligent, conscious entity, is in the realm of scientific philosophy and logic. The nature of a God who exists is mostly in the realm of theology.

Traditional Christian theology would acknowledge that God does allow pain and suffering. But God didn't create it. It is the result of sin. It is similar to you allowing your kid to ride the bike. Your child crashes and gets hurt. Is that your fault? If you apply that kind of thinking to God, then yes, it is your fault. As far as I know all religious ideologies contain the hope or promise of a life or being that is free of pain and suffering. Maybe you become God, reach Nirvana, or become part of the cosmic consciousness.

Imagine with me for a moment. If you were able to create a life form that you desired to love you, would you create a robot that had no choice but to do that which it was programmed to do? If you've had children, you love them and want them to love you. You also don't want them to have any harm. Would you therefore want them to be like the bubble boy? I think not. You do your best and wish them the best. You teach them, you watch over them as you can, and you hope for the best. But if they are only responding in ways that appropriate love, where it is not a choice, it cannot be fulfilling to you. Sometimes you tell your child something you know he or she will not like. You think it is in their best interest. You hope your child takes your advice and doesn't hate you. Still, you don't know. Your child doesn't know that you are trying your best to guide them. If you turn your child lose on a bicycle and they break an arm, is that your fault? If you stub your toe and trip and break a rib, is that God's fault? You get my drift?

This may be a bit redundant, but an important point to me. Bottom line is, if there is a creator, there is a creator. If you don't like anything or everything about that creator -- too bad. You can choose to not believe in or to ignore that creator, but that has nothing to do with whether or not there is that creator. If you are a painter and you paint a picture, you are the designing painter of the picture. The picture can't say that it doesn't like the way it looks or the painter. But because we have been endowed with some intelligence and free will, we can ask some of those questions. It's okay to ask, but ultimately worse than jousting at windmills.

Some say that we humans are so imperfect that we could not be beings created by God. Some have used our eyes as an example. They have said that the eye is full of functional design flaws. Others see our eyes as amazingly functional parts of our bodies. Some have said that God isn't that smart to put excretory functions so close to reproductive parts. We are what we are. Pardon me for this, but given who we are, where would you put your anus? On the bottom of your foot, so you walk around stepping on your butt. Or, on your belly? That might make hugging a bit messy, no?

I know a blind man. He is bright and a believer. He sings in the choir. As he is single, someone asked him about dating or girls in his life. He responded that he had dated. The person asked him about what if the girl was ugly. I will never forget his answer. He said, "What is ugly?" How profound. While seeing, we can be blind to beauty. While knowing something, we can be ignorant of truth.

I have to add here that such things are easier for me to deal with from a Christian perspective. From a Christian theological perspective there are angels created by God. They had free will and some decided they would like to be like God, free of God, do their own thing. The leader of the group we call Satan, the devil. His followers we call demons. Because they rebelled against God, they like us humans to rebel against God. They influence us to do ungodly things that cause us problems that we then blame on God.

NON-THEISTS BECOMING THEISTS AND VICE VERSA

S ome atheists and agnostics change their beliefs and embrace belief in the existence of something that is responsible for our being here; something that could be called god. Likewise, some theists lose faith in god. In regard to my reasons for believing, I am more interested in the former. Although reasons for people losing faith are also interesting. In the following I share a couple of examples of people who rejected their atheism or agnosticism. Then I mention some examples of Christians who, as they say, deconverted. Also, I share some personal information.

First, some people who converted to theism. Not all converts to theism are also converted to Christianity. Within Christianity, a convert to Christianity is often spoken of as becoming saved. Each person has their own reasons for and experience of conversion. The telling of the personal conversion is referred to as sharing one's testimony. Everyone's testimony is in some way unique to that person and as important as any other. The one's I'm mentioning were selected because of the person being well-known or having philosophical or scientific credentials. I do so because it seems common for many agnostics/atheists to take it for granted that belief in God is below anyone of any sense or intelligence.

C. S. Lewis   You may know of C. S. Lewis as the author of *The Chronicles of Narnia* or his science fiction trilogy of *Out of the Silent Planet*, *Perelandra* and *That Hideous Strength*. He was a Felllow and

Tutor in English Literature at Oxford University and served as Chair of Medieval and Renaissance Literature at Cambridge University. He rejected Christianity in his early teens and lived as an atheist through his 20's. During this time, he primarily considered himself a materialist, while also having great interest in the occult. In his book, *Surprised by Joy*, he writes: "Several years before I read Lucretius I felt the force of his argument (and it is surely the strongest of all) for atheism—'Had God designed the world, it would not be, A world so frail and faulty as we see.' You may ask how I combined this directly Atheistical thought, this great "Argument from Undesign" with my Occultist fancies. I do not think I achieved any logical connection between them. They swayed me in different moods, and had only this in common, that both made against Christianity. And so, little by little, with fluctuations which I cannot now trace, I became an apostate, dropping my faith with no sense of loss but with the greatest relief." (Lewis 1955, 78-79)

Lewis converted to theism when he was 32. A year or two later, partly with encouragement to openness by two Christian friends, one being J. R. R. Tolkien, he converted to Christianity. He authored over thirty books, many dealing with matters of faith and Christian philosophy.

Hugh Ross, Ph.D. Dr. Ross did undergraduate studies in physics at the University of British Columbia, received his graduate degree in astronomy at the University of Toronto, and did post-doctoral research at California Institute of Technology. Writing of his journey towards faith, he said, "Discoveries in astronomy first alerted me to the existence of God, and to this day the Bible's unfathomable depths, predictive power, and remarkable applicability to life rank as major reasons for my faith." [from My Story: Dr. Hugh Ross, at www.cru. org]

Lee Strobel Lee received a Master in Law degree from Yale. He was a journalist and legal editor with the Chicago Tribune. His book, *The Case for Christ*, is primarily about his conversion. The following is his own statement taken from washred.com, titled Lee Strobel's Testimony: An Atheist Investigates Christianity. "For most of my life I was an atheist. I thought the idea of an all-loving, all-powerful creator of the universe--I thought it was stupid. I mean, my background is in journalism and law. I tend to be a skeptical person. I was the legal editor of the Chicago Tribune. So I needed evidence before I'd believe anything." Furthermore, he wrote the following.

"One day my wife came up to me--she'd been agnostic--and she said after a period of spiritual investigation she had decided to become a follower of Jesus Christ. And I thought, you know, this is the worst possible news I could get. I thought she was going to turn into some sexually repressed prude who was going to spend all her time serving the poor in skid row somewhere. I thought this was the end of our marriage.

But in the ensuing months, I saw positive changes in her values, in her character, in the way she related to me and the children. It was winsome; and it was attractive; and it made me want to check things out. So I went to church one day, ah, mainly to see if I could get her out of this cult that she had gotten involved in.

But I heard the message of Jesus articulated for the first time in a way that I could understand it. That forgiveness is a free gift, and that Jesus Christ died for our sins, that we might spend eternity with Him. And I walked out saying--I was still an atheist--but also saying, 'If this is true, this has huge implications for my life.' And so I used my journalism training and legal training to begin an investigation into whether there was any credibility to Christianity or to any other world faith system for that matter.

I did that for a year and nine months until November the 8th of 1991, and on that day I realized that, in light of the torrent of evidence flowing in the direction of the truth of Christianity, it would require more faith for me to maintain my atheism than to become a Christian. Because to be an atheist I would have to swim upstream against this torrent of evidence pointing toward the truth of Jesus Christ. And I couldn't do that. I was trained in journalism and law to respond to truth. And so on that day, I received Jesus Christ as my forgiver, and as my leader."

<u>Josh McDowell</u>   Josh was an agnostic and considered Christianity worthless. After studying the evidence, he converted to Christianity. He wrote *Evidence that Demands a Verdict: Life Changing Truth for a Skeptical World.*

<u>Francis Collins</u>   Dr. Collins was an atheist through much of his life. He has a B.S. in chemistry from the University of Virginia, Ph.D. in physical chemistry from Yale, and M.D. from the University of North Carolina at Chapel Hill. He served as director of the National Human Genome Research Institute and the National Institutes of Health. He is the author of *The Language of God: A Scientist Presents Evidence for Belief.*

<u>William J. Murry</u>   Bill is the son of the atheist activist Madalyn Murry O'Hair. He was listed as a plaintiff in her suit, which became Abington School District v. Schempp, to remove mandatory Bible reading from schools. He became a Christian at age 34. After that his mother said, "One could call this postnatal abortion on the part of a mother, I guess; I repudiate him entirely and completely for now and all times. He is beyond human forgiveness." He wrote *My Life Without God* (Harvest House Publishers, 1982.) [from Wikipedia, quote attributed to: Dracos, Ted (2003), *UnGodly: The Passions, Torments, and Murder of Atheist Madalyn Murray O'Hair*, Free Press, p.138]

<u>Allan Sandage</u>   Dr. Sandage was a prominent astronomer of the 20th century. He received an undergraduate degree from the University of Illinois and Ph.D. from California Institute of Technology. He became a Christian at age 57. He said, "I could not live a life full of cynicism. I chose to believe, and a peace of mind came over me." [Wikipedia]

<u>Antony Flew</u>   Flew was an atheist for most of his life and was a champion for atheism. One of his more influential books was *The Presumption of Atheism* (1976). As a result of following the evidence he became a theist (deist) in 2004. He explains his change in position in his book, *There is a God: How the world's most notorious atheist changed his mind.*

<u>Mortimer J. Adler</u>   Some of you may know him as the author of *How to Read a Book*. He was a prolific author. I enjoyed his *Aristotle for Everybody*, but admit it was far from an easy read for this everybody. Before accepting Christianity, he said that there were "moral, not intellectual obstacles to his conversion." After his conversion he stated, "My chief reason for choosing Christianity was because the mysteries were incomprehensible. What's the point of revelation if we could figure it out ourselves? If it were wholly comprehensible, then it would just be another philosophy." [from biographybase.com]

Mark Farner   I have to mention Mark, being an old Grand Funk Railroad fan. Mark is one who strayed from the faith of his youth for years. Later he returned to faith. I heard him tell, during a concert in 2017, how he died and saw heaven. [MarkFarner.com and Mark at Sangamon State Auditorium, 2/11/2017.] His story is told in the book, *From Grand Funk to Grace: The authorized biography of Mark Farner* by Kristofer Englehardt.

Now I'd like to share some examples of Christian theists who deconverted to atheism or agnosticism. It seems to me that in many ways reasons for non-theists becoming theists are the same as for theists becoming non-theists in reverse. For some it is a search for truth. For some it is because of something in life or their life that they like or don't like. The following examples are taken from allernet.com.

<u>Teresa MacBain</u>   Teresa was a minister for many years. She stated, "I didn't want to lose my faith. I didn't want to change or stop believing, but I wanted truth more."

<u>Jerry DeWitt</u>   Jerry was born in 1969 and served as pastor of two evangelical churches. He deconverted in 2011. He wrote: *Hope After Faith*. He stated, "Skepticism is my nature. Free thought is my methodology. Agnosticism is my conclusion. Humanitarianism is my motivation."

<u>Anthony Pinn, Ph.D.</u>   Dr. Pinn began preaching at age twelve. He obtained a Ph.D. in religious studies from Harvard. In regard to his current beliefs, he stated, "I think African Americans are worse off because of their allegiance to theism. The belief in God and gods has

not been particularly useful or productive tor them. It has lessened their appeal to their own creativity and ingenuity, and in most cases has resulted in a kind of bizarre understanding of suffering as a marker of closeness to God and a mark of divine favor. Nothing good can come out of that."

<u>Dan Burke</u>   Dan was a preacher and Christian musician. In 1984 he announced that he was an atheist. He said, "How happy can you be when you think every action and thought is being monitored by a judgmental ghost?"

<u>Frank Schaeffer</u>   Frank is the son of Francis Schaeffer, a well-known Christian author. Frank was active as a speaker and film maker in evangelical circles earlier in his life. I mention him because of the uniqueness of his professed belief, which is presented in his book, *Why I am an Atheist Who Believes in God*. He was a Christian theist. Now he is not a Christian, but an atheist and theist. In his own words, "These days I hold two ideas about God simultaneously; he, she or it exists and he, she or it doesn't exist. I don't seesaw between these opposites; I embrace them." (Schaeffer 2014, 13) I can't make any sense of that. Theist and Atheist are antithetical. Seems to me to say that someone is both is oxymoronic. Frank is satisfied to call it a paradox. I guess that it is only because of his understanding of this paradox that he can make statements like the following.

"Maybe we need a new category other than theism, atheism or agnosticism that takes paradox and unknowing into account. I believe that life evolved by natural selection. I believe that evolutionary psychology explains away altruism and debunks love and that brain chemistry undermines my illusion of free will and personhood. I also believe that the spiritual reality hovering over, in and through me calls me to love, trust and hear the voice of my Creator." (Schaeffer 2014, 15)

"My brain is not evolved enough to reconcile the collision of my genetic imperative with transcendent experience. My brain recognizes but can't explain how love and beauty intersect with the prime directive of evolution: survive. Nor can I reconcile these ideas: 'I know that the only thing that exists is this material universe.' And 'I know that my redeemer liveth.'" (Schaeffer 2014, 7)

"Scientists have found direct evidence of the expansion of the universe, a previously theoretical event that took place a fraction of a second after the Big Bang nearly 14 billion years ago. The clue is encoded in the primordial cosmic microwave background radiation that continues to spread. My hope is that a trillionth of a second before the Big Bang, the energy animating the mystery of matter being created out of nothing was love." (Schaeffer 2014,139)

Well, seems Frank went from being a Christian theist to considering himself an atheist & theist. What then is the answer to the question in the title of his father's book, *How Should We Then Live?*

Me I was a Christian who became a weak theist; basically, stepped away from my Christian faith. This was after three years of Bible college and years of serving in my church as youth group sponsor and deacon. There are always reasons why a Christian has doubts or struggles with their faith. Understanding mine was part of my returning to faith. I had some kind of idea that if I had lived a certain way that God would bless a part of my life. That part of my life fell apart. I blamed God. I drifted away from my faith. I considered myself a quasi-agnostic deist. Like, there's probably a God but we don't have much to do with each other. Then my twenty-one-year-old son died. That didn't affect where I was in terms of my faith. But the person who mentored me in the faith originally showed up at the funeral. We'd been out of touch for years. I was glad to see him. I started some deep reflection and realized that my disappointment in God and anger at him were based on my faulty expectations. And then I was dating my wife, who invited me to church with her. All in all, my faith is restored.

You know that I believe in free will. With our mind and consciousness, we are able to make choices. Our choices are based on information, with processing of the information, experiences, and emotion. At any point in time, a choice may be more strongly influenced by any of these factors.

Some will say that the only reason you believe this or that is because of the circumstances of your upbringing—the country in which you were born, the family in to which you were born and the beliefs of that family and your psychosocial culture. I believe there is a lot of truth to that, yet people change with information and experience, as shown in above examples.

Outside of a couple years of Bible college, my education background is psychology, mostly social psychology. I remember the studies of how regular folk changed in different situations as presented in *The Social Animal*. I can attest to the power of social setting and peer pressure and group joining behavior. For reasons I'll spare you, I was in a thirty-day residential treatment facility. I know that the psychosocial forces, including peer pressure, to conform can be tremendous. As are certain "brain-washing" methods. However true, such truths don't fully encompass the concept of choice.

For years, I struggled with the concept of how you would be different if you grew up differently. I now think that as stated that would be true but it is an impossible event. If "I" was born to different parents, in a different country, that would not be me. I am not a me that could have been born to parents here or there. Some of you may think that you were a soul waiting to be born or reincarnated, but I don't believe I was.

Regardless, it is a choice. Maybe it's not as much of a choice when we're our younger. At some point we realize it is a choice. We see that people choose to be atheists or theists and that they can choose to change their choice. My point is, that to me, my choice to believe in God is at least every bit as reasonable as choosing to not believe in God.

THEOLOGY SUPPORTS MY BELIEF

Originally, I was going to write what is contained in the following about how the Biblical witness supports my belief. But I realize that you may not relate to the Bible in ways that I do. The Bible is not necessary to my being a theist. Neither is Christian theology. But both do, in my understanding, support my belief in God.

What is *theology* anyway? It is described as "the study of the nature of God and religious belief, religious beliefs when systematically developed." We cannot actually study the nature of God. We study what philosophers and theologians have written about the nature of God. It is largely a study of studies with maybe some new take on this or that aspect or how some things do or don't go together. I could be wrong, but I don't think there are any or many college classes like Theology 101. There could be an Introduction to Theology class. Such a course would introduce us to thoughts about God or a supreme being by classic philosophers, early Jewish/Hebrew literature, the Bible, Buda, Mohammed, eastern philosophies, etc. This might be something like a comparative religions class.

Regardless of the emphasis, the studies are based on writings and writings about those writings. Christian theology is based on the Bible, early Jewish/Hebrew writings, writings of early and contemporary Christian theologians and others. Similar to ways that other religions draw their theology from writings of people they revere, including prophets and religious leaders.

Christian theology, which is primarily based on information contained in the Bible, has some implicit assumptions. If there is a God who created us people, it is sensible that He would reveal Himself to us. The Bible is both a record of this revelation and a revelation in and of itself.

I'll say a couple things in these regards and continue. There are many scholarly and too many popular books that discuss the historicity of the Bible, literary criticism, inerrancy, infallibility, etc. having to do with the Bible. I attempt to summarize the major aspects of those things that add to reasons I believe.

The Bible is not a history book. As far as I can tell, the more that is known, from contemporary writings and archeology, the more the Bible is shown to be historically accurate. The Bible is not a scientific text. But the more that's known, it is more consistent with known science.

The main thing that the Bible and Christian theology helps me with has to do with the concept of sin and its effect on everything. You might not believe in sin. Let me say the following and think about it philosophically.

This is based on some assumptions. You might not, but I accept the assumptions, so the rest makes logical sense to me. One assumption is that there is sin and at the simplest level, sin is to act differently than what God wants. Or, trying to be like God by thinking that you are the source of your morality. Some Biblical scholars have said that sin is missing the mark. Like in playing darts, the goal is to hit a bullseye. I say it may be more like making your own bullseye, one that isn't God's.

The majority of Christian theologians have always held that sin disrupted the relationship between God and man. It also affected the whole of creation. One reason the world is messed up is because of sin and continued sinning. I know, that sounds like a cop out. But follow this line of thinking. A woman suffered death because someone made a choice to kill her. That could be rewritten as: a woman suffered death because someone chose to sin by killing her. Biblically, things like hate and greed are sinful. If you add to that pride, jealousy, gossip, coveting, lust, and holding a grudge, you can see how sin affects human life in general. I hope you get the gist of that.

In the first verse of the first book of the Bible, it says that in the beginning God created heaven and earth. Elsewhere, it is written that God sustains creation. It also describes God as being a supreme, autonomous, intelligent, and external (in terms of time and matter) spiritual being. That all fits with the need for a creator.

There is a question about God, both theological and philosophical, regarding the nature of His character. This is usually framed in this way, if God is good by nature, then it doesn't matter what He does, it is good. So, aren't we lucky that He is good? And, if He is good, why is there evil? The question only indirectly questions the existence of God.

In the Biblical book of Isiah, Yahweh (God) says: "Woe to anyone who argues with his Maker, one earthenware pot among many! Does the clay say to the potter, 'What are you doing?'" (Isiah 45:19) A related thought is implicit in this statement to believers: "You believe in the one God—that is creditable enough, but even the demons have the same faith, and they tremble with fear." (James 2:19)

Finally, the Bible is blatantly forthcoming about sin and our lives. It tells of how God directed the killing of people. Yes, life is precious. That is clear throughout scripture. Yet, life is not the ultimate good thing above everything else.

The Bible is open about good and evil. And it is brutally honest. I like this verse, which says regarding believers: "If our hope in Christ has been for this life only, we are of all people the most pitiable." (I Corinthians 15:19)

RANDOM THOUGHTS ON ALIENS, SPIRITS AND EVOLUTION

Honestly, I am rather amused by all the interest in aliens or extraterrestrial intelligent life. I doubt that intelligent alien life forms exist, at least that we'll ever be in touch with. But it doesn't make any difference to me one way or the other. I do watch shows that present and discuss evidence for ET. Although some of it is compelling, much is highly speculative, and some seems to be simply entertainment. And, I do like the movies ET, Star Trek, Star Wars, and things of that genre.

I do believe that there are some things referred to as Unidentified Flying Objects, or UFOs. And, if they're not objects, Unidentified Arial Phenomenon (UAP). After all, there is a government agency that studies such. The Unidentified Arial Phenomenon Task Force (UAPTF) operates as part of the U.S. Office of Naval Intelligence. Whatever it is, it could be natural events or military something or alien objects. I find it interesting and a little bit funny that there is a project to contact aliens, the SETI project (Search for Extraterrestrial Intelligence). I don't know what the purpose of that project is if we have already had contact and they are here. There is also a project working on what to do when we make first contact. This is the SETI Post-Detection Hub at the University of St. Andrews in Scotland. I don't understand the existence of that either if we have had contact and they are among us. Some people say they have seen aliens, some say they have been abducted, some say they have been at Site 51 and there were aliens there. I can not say they are wrong. I don't think there's enough evidence to say they are right. I am dubious.

There is an equation many refer to estimate the number of detectable civilizations in the Milky Way. It uses 7 variables (and more are needed). The variables relate to planet conditions such as temperature, rockiness, having orbiting sunlike stars, etc. The Drake Equation indicates there may be many in the Milky Way. The closest is about 20 light years away. Nadia Drake worked with her father on the equation. She said, "But working out those last variables in the Drake Equation – the ones that will tell us whether Earth is home to the galaxy's only technologically adept organisms – will be mysteries until, as my father says, we've heard the murmurings of alien worlds." (naturalgeograpic.com/science/2020/10…)

By the time you're reading this, there will surely be more sightings and theories about these things and the government may have issued a report about such. The most interesting thing that I've come across recently is that outside of maneuvering in ways we can't technologically replicate, whatever it was seemed to travel faster than the speed of sound without breaking the sound barrier. Hear tell that we have no clue as to how that could be done. Aliens are a plausible answer.

Still, I don't understand the desire to discover or be discovered by aliens to prove that we are not alone in the universe. Really? You are one among all the other humans on the planet, and to know that aliens exist will make you feel that you are not alone?

If there are aliens, it seems obvious that they would discover us before we would discover them. Maybe not, if they were either less intelligent or technologically advanced than we are. If aliens have already visited us, they are evidently more technologically advanced and more intelligent than humans. One commentator said that we need to know who they are and what their intent is. That's hilarious. If it's aliens, don't you think they could contact us if they wanted to?

However, there is some excitement about identifying that the closest habitable planet may be only 20 light years away. That is close in astronomical terms. The observable universe is said to be 93 billion light years in diameter, and expanding. But, it's good to keep things in perspective.

One light year is roughly 5.9 trillion miles. Twenty light years is around 118 trillion miles. Last I've heard, we can travel 450,000 miles per hour in space. If my math is correct, at 500 thousand miles per hour it would take over twenty-six thousand years to get there. And, since radio waves travel around the speed of light, it would take 20 years to receive communication. Not to say that such may be possible some time maybe, but it definitely won't be tomorrow.

Perhaps there are worm holes. Their existence is still mostly theoretical. But if they exist, it is also theoretical that they are something that could be navigable. As in have space craft that could do it and knowledge enough to control where one goes to. Could happen, but it won't be tomorrow either. Recently I've read that warp speed may be possible. Going faster than the speed of light. It would require the bending of space time and negative energy, which there is no idea of how to do. And, it might take more negative energy than there is in the universe. The newer idea is to create a bubble in space time that "travels" in a way like quantum particles. Meaning that the bubble would go where it goes. Not even any theoretical idea I know of as to how to control your "flight." These ideas are based on theoretical astrophysical mathematics. Perhaps it could be possible. But there is no science, at least of any significance, that says such would ever even be possible. To think so is a belief in science. That's OK. I have some belief in hoping science can accomplish many things. Say, cure the common cold and then cancer and then ….

If aliens have already been here, they are incontrovertibly of higher technology and intelligence than earthlings. Some say they created humans. Some say they came to help humans. If either or both of those things are true, it doesn't answer the question as to where then did the aliens come from. If they came to help us, it doesn't seem to me that they are all that intelligent after all. I've imagined a scenario in which humans and aliens communicate. The humans ask the aliens about the existence of the universe. The aliens respond that some of their scientists think it came from nothing and others believe it is the creation of an autonomous, intelligent entity. Wouldn't that be a hoot!

I believe that the universe and all that was made was made for the existence of us human people. If it was also made for others like aliens, then it was. I think there's enough room. But I believe we are alone except for each other (and maybe alone with aliens) and our creator.

In the book *Improbable Planet*, Ross presents a number of reasons why earth and its place in our galaxy are uniquely equipped to provide for life. These are mostly beyond my comprehension. Basically, there are conditions that are necessary for the existence of certain elements in certain proportions and not others, it has to be a spiral galaxy, things need to be the right size, there needs to be no super galaxies in the larger galaxy family, there has to be a sufficient number but not too many dwarf galaxies, etc. After presenting these conditions, he states the following.

"The observations and explorations provide a framework within which we can consider the implications of such an amazing multiplex of coincidences. While we have much to learn and understand, a strong suggestion of intentionality and purpose has clearly emerged. As physicist Freeman Dyson wrote in his book *Disturbing the Universe*, 'The more I examine the universe and study the details of its architecture, the more evidence I find that the universe in some sense must have known we were coming.'" (Ross 2016, 42)

Regarding extraterrestrial intelligence, Hawking wrote the following. "Perhaps intelligence was an unlikely development for life on Earth, from the chronology of evolution, as it took a very long time – two and a half billion years – to go from single cells to multi-cellular beings. Which are a necessary precursor to intelligence. This is a good fraction of the total time available before the sun blows up, so it would be consistent with the hypothesis that the probability for life to develop intelligence is low. In this case, we might expect to find many other life forms in the galaxy, but we are unlikely to find intelligent life." (Hawking 2018, 84)

John Gibben, who wrote a whole book about humans being alone in this universe wrote the following. "The reasons we are here form a chain so improbable that the chance of any other technological civilization existing in the Milky Way Galaxy at the present time is vanishingly small. We are alone, and we had better get used to the idea." (Gibben 2011, 105)

And finally, a sort of humorous thought that I can half-way to relate to from Hawking. "Meeting a more advanced civilization, at our present age might be a bit like the original inhabitants of America meeting Columbus – and I don't think they thought they were better off for it." (Hawking 2018, 86)

Here's different thought that I've only come across recently. The idea is that God, who created many spiritual beings, created "gods." These gods were put in control of different parts of the earth with certain spiritual powers. Like angels, some if not all of them, abused their power by wanting to be like God. They injected their selves in to human life to get praise for themselves rather than to serve God and give Him the glory. In this regard, the human god's (like Zeus) may have been gods. [Attention to upper- & lower-case God or gods is important here.] Hence, God is above all gods. There is only one God, who created all else that is. The idea here is that God created divine beings that you could call (lower case) gods. In the book of Job there is a presentation of questions that God offers to Job. God asks Job many questions that rhetorically illustrate how Job doesn't have any right or justification to question God. God speaks about His creation of earth. One of the questions is as follows. "Who laid its cornerstone to the joyful concert of the morning stars and unanimous acclaim of the sons of God" (Job 38:6 – 7) These "sons of God" were present with God as He created the earth. These "gods" may have been responsible for things that ancient alien theorists talk about. I find this interesting but don't have any opinion. (If you have interest in these thoughts. I refer you to two books by Michael S. Heiser: *Super Natural* and *The Unseen Realm*)

Evolution is often offered as evidence that there is no God. It is suggested that, given evolution, there is no need God. It could be an argument that a god is not necessary for the creation of life or people.

Still, there is evidence that an external, intelligent, autonomous entity may be or is necessary for the creation of the universe. In that sense, evolution has nothing to do with whether there is a god.

I have struggled with trying to reconcile evolution with my Judeo-Christian beliefs. I wish I had a better understanding but I am content with my thoughts about such at the moment. It's obvious that things evolve, meaning that they change. In some way, no matter how little, most things change. As far as I know, the basic elements don't change, evolve. There doesn't appear to be a variant of oxygen. Oxygen doesn't evolve.

My current understanding is not that God just like that created Adam and Eve. Although I believe He could have. There are many scholarly writings dealing with the creation/evolution issue. The major questions I've had are about the making of each beast after its own kind and the Adam and Eve thing. But all of that has nothing to do with believing in God. It is about the theology concerning how God did all of those things. The major problems arise with efforts to reconcile the Biblical account with science. There are many ideas and I have mine. I believe that, in one way or another, God created everything including us people.

I do a little study in this area off and on. One idea that interests me has to do with the word *day* in the Biblical account of creation. According to some Hebrew scholars that does not necessarily refer to a 24-hour period. It can refer to a period of time. Likewise, the number of hours between night and day may have been much different during the earlier days of creation. And, the creation story may be a story. In literary type terms this is where the material is not completely fact (as in scientific fact), nor is it fiction. It is a way of passing on information about something that happened. I have no problem thinking that God created the matter of the universe and then used that matter to make everything in the universe. That would include intervening in evolutionary processes to produce human beings that are made in His image. Perhaps that's all that was necessary. I don't think that's a leap for anyone who thinks that God intervenes on account of prayer or His own will. It is complicated to me. I don't think this prevents a historical Adam and Eve. At some point God may be pleased with the creation of a being called Adam. And, then, somehow from him God creates Eve. I'm okay with thinking that God used the same materials as used with Adam or that He made Eve from a rib of Adam or that is a story to share what God has done.

I do believe that humans, being made in the image of God, are different than other living things in the universe. Theologians and philosophers have pondered this issue for a long time and written more than I could read in my life time. Here's my brief take on these considerations. I believe that God gave life to living things. I believe that there is something else that one might call a soul. And, the soul is given to humans, and it with our spiritual nature comprises our being in the image of God. There are philosophical and theological thoughts that classify things as inanimate matter, living beings, soulful beings, and humans who are made in the image of God.

This is why we can step on a worm and feel no or little remorse. If we drive the car over a cat, we can feel sad. The idea is that a worm is living, but it is not a soulful being. We can interact in some ways with the cat, same as a dog and other beings. Still, we can eat a dog or cat. Or a cow. A soulful being is not a human being. However, the Bible is clear that we humans are to care for the earth and not to abuse other living beings. If I was in one of those movies where some others had died and I was starving, I think I might eat them. I would not kill them to eat them.

My Native American ancestors and some contemporaries might say something like walk gently on the grass, we are all related. At least in some sense, I believe that is true. Someone might kill a deer for food and pelt. Yet, give thanks to the great spirit and the spirit of the deer for those provisions. And, that makes sense to me. Some spiritual leaders may give thanks for every drink of water. I am not that spiritual, but that also makes sense to me.

I believe in spirits. After all, God is spirit. I believe we are too. I believe God made many spiritual beings. The one most of us think of are angels. I mentioned my belief that some angels rebelled against God, and were thrown out of heaven. The leader was Lucifer, now known as Satan. He and his followers we call demons. The existence of demons, if you believe in them, is evidence for God. The word for angel comes from Greek, meaning a messenger. Angels speak for God. Demons speak for the devil. If you believe in one, I don't know how you wouldn't also believe in the other.

Speaking of spirits, there are people who seek to talk to the dead. Obviously, they believe that there is life after death. Which means they believe that we are more than just matter. How is it that we are beings that have life after our death? Perhaps because of the God who created us to relate to us. I do not doubt that such can be done. I must say that I don't think it is something that one should seek to do. It is said to be something not to do in the Bible. I think the major reason is that in our current state at least most of us cannot discern between the spirit of a dead family member over that of an imitating demon. We just aren't smart enough or spiritual enough.

I believe that there are many things we don't understand about the spiritual, and even natural, reality in which we exist. It is a kind of belief to think that science will eventually provide an understanding of everything. You could say that the evidence is actually the opposite. The more we know, the more we know how much we don't know. Simple example: we thought there were three states of matter – solid, liquid and gas. Then, there's plasma. And now, maybe swirlon. Well, as smart as we like to think we are, scientists are working to solve or discover a hundred more things before going after another thousand or more things.

I BELIEVE IN GOD THE FATHER, SON, HOLY SPIRIT

If you haven't believed in God, I hope you consider reasons to do so. If you believe in God, I hope you consider that His interaction and revelation is given to us in the Bible. And, in the Bible you might find that Jesus is the son of God, who is God with the father and the holy spirit, in whom I believe and are therefore saved to live with God forever.

I believe in God, the Father, Son and Holy Spirit. I can't comprehend what is called the Trinity. I believe what is recorded for us in the bible. Christmas is about Christ. Jesus of Nazareth. I only know of these things from the Holy Bible. I believe the Bible is one way God reveals himself to us today by a recording of how he revealed himself to people in the past. It is one way as is natural revelation (beauty, science, etc.) and philosophy.

I know that there are questions about what is historical and about this and that and timelines and such. I am not going to go into all that stuff. I am going to say that from all that I know and have studied I still have as much (if not more) reason to believe in the Christian God than not. You may not agree, I respect that. If you are interested you can further study for yourself. There are tons of tomes on these subjects. I am no expert. I believe that I am open and will examine any new thing that challenges my belief. No body can examine everything, right?

I believe there is a God. I believe God created all that is. That includes me and you.. It is not necessary, but it makes sense that if God created people, he may interact with them. I believe that we learn much about that from the Old Testament. We learn more from the New Testament. As a result of all I know I continue to believe in God the Father, Son, and Holy Spirit. Among all who claimed to be prophets and such, outside of the obviously crazies, only Jesus claimed to be the son of God and by other statements claiming to be God. I believe in his historical reality, his crucifixion and resurrection. [A technical presentation may be found in Goothuis, Chapter 19, Jesus of Nazareth: How Historians Can Know Him and Why It Matters.]

I believe there are many prophecies in the Old Testament that told of the virgin birth and Emmanuel (God with us). I believe the first disciples of Jesus suffered painful deaths at the hands of anti-Christians. I know people of other faiths have too. I believe that the Biblical theology of sin explains most or all of our problems. God is my creator and he cares for me. He gives me instructions. Have any of you parents not heard your child at one time say to you: You are not the boss of me? God is not our boss and we are not the boss of our children. The instruction we give is for their good because we love them. God is our maker and gives us instruction for our good and salvation. There were writers contemporary with the New Testament writers. As far as I know there were none who challenged the writings about the crucifixion and resurrection of Jesus.

C. S. Lewis wrote the following. "A man who was merely a man and said the sort of things that Jesus said would not be a great moral teacher. He would either be a lunatic – on a level with the man who says he is a poached egg – or else he would be the Devil of Hell. You must make your choice. Either this man was, and is, the Son of God: or else a madman or something worse. You can shut Him up for a fool, you can spit at Him and kill Him as a demon; or you can fall at

His feet and call Him Lord and God. But let us not come with any patronizing nonsense about His being a great human teacher. He has not left that open to us. He did not intend to." (Lewis, 1970, 289)

Christians have messed up in a lot of ways. (And also have other faiths,) That makes me sad. However, they have also been a source of good. Much of charitable good comes from Christians.

I don't apologize for what I'm about to say. If you understand historic Judeo-Christian faith, you understand that no one comes to the Father except through the Son. There are not many ways to be saved. There is one God. You may believe differently; I know most do. Do an honest comparison of any belief with Christianity. If you seek truth, I believe you will find that they are not compatible as different ways to be saved and be with God.

There are many popular books about how there are many ways to get to God. Interesting though, that the definition of "God" isn't the Judeo-Christian God. So, all of that fails to get off the starting line.

An example is a popular book by Thich Nhat Hanh, *Living Buddha, Living Christ*. In the book it states: "You are born in your tradition, and naturally you become a Buddhist or a Christian. Buddhism or Christianity is part of your culture and civilization. You are familiar with your culture and appreciate the good things in it. You may not be aware that in other cultures and civilizations there are value that people are attached to. If you are open enough, you will understand that your tradition does not contain all truths and values. It is easy to get caught in the idea that salvation is not possible outside of your tradition. A deep and correct practice of your tradition may release you from that dangerous belief."

Pardon me, but the Buddhist idea of salvation is not like a Christian one. And, I am interested in why my belief is a dangerous one. Perhaps a deep and correct practice and study of your tradition may lead you to Jesus.

Can't we be friends with people we disagree with on what we consider the most important thing in life? Of course, we can. We share. We chose and so do they. May we all pray and God have mercy on us all.

I believe there is a God. I believe God created all that is. That includes me and you. It is not necessary, but it makes sense that if God created people, he may interact with them. I believe that there is a God. I believe God created all that is. That includes me and you. It is not necessary, but it makes sense that if God created people, he may interact with them. I believe that we learn much about that from the Old Testament. We learn more from the New Testament. As a result of all I know I continue to believe in God the Father, Son, and Holy Spirit. Among all who claimed to be prophets and such, outside of the obviously crazies, only Jesus claimed to be the son of God and by other statements claiming to be God. I believe in his historical reality, his crucifixion and resurrection.

Christians have messed up in a lot of ways. (And also have other faiths,) That makes me sad. However, they have also been a source of good. Much of charitable good comes from Christians.

CLOSING COMMENTS

In concluding, I believe there are many reasons to believe in God. I believe that belief in God is plausible and makes as much sense scientifically and philosophically as to not believe. I know, my reasons are debatable and you may disagree. I believe that ultimately, it is a choice and matter of faith based on evidence.

I ask myself, how can there be a God? My answer is always another question, how can there not be? I believe that an autonomous, intelligent, external (outside and yet inside) of our time something (which I believe is the God of the Bible), is either necessary or at least a possible explanation for the complexities of the material world and existence of the metaphysical realities.

Personally, I cannot handle or deal with the idea that there is a God who has also been as I've stated in this book. It hurts me. I cannot ponder it. It is intellectually as one might say painful to death. Yet, I'd feel no different if I was struggled with how could matter just be there. If you relate you know it existentially rips your guts.

After hosting a radio talk show for more than ten years that brought together prominent atheists and Christians to discuss various topics, Justin Brierley wrote a book about why he's still a Christian. Part of his reason he states as follows. "The case for God is a cumulative one that reaches well beyond science alone .... But on the balance of all I see so far, I cannot reconcile myself to believing that humanity is simply the accidental by-product of an undirected and unpurposed universe that came from nowhere and is heading into oblivion. I also cannot escape a conviction that the order, elegance and majesty of the universe and our existence within it is crying out for an explanation beyond itself. Atheism cannot account for such a world. That's why God is the best explanation for human existence." (Brierley 2017, 50)

I don't believe that matter has always existed or comes from nothing. I believe that God created the universe and sustains it (keeps it from falling apart). Within that understanding, it seems that eventually things will fall apart sometime in the far distant future. I believe that God will return some time to redeem creation. There are a lot of takes as to what that might mean. What that might mean don't matter to me, I believe it will be.

I don't believe that all of the amazingly complex functions and interactions and things necessary for existence and function are the result of an accident or good luck. I believe there is strong evidence of design and that God is the designer.

I don't believe that consciousness, intelligence, or free will came from non-living, non-conscious matter. I believe that life itself, and these things were imparted by God.

I don't believe that a concept of morality or feelings of emotions came from matter. I believe that God is the source of absolute truth and, hence, right and wrong. I also believe that God is the only one who is completely full of justice and righteousness as well as mercy and forgiveness.

I don't believe that just because pain exists, or that people have done evil, even in the name of religion, that it is evidence that God doesn't exist. It is also true that much good is done by believers. I believe that these things make logical sense in light of Judeo-Christian theology.

There are also our personal experiences. This is obviously very subjective. I am cautious about any dealing with this subject. It is another of those things that is quite complicated. We know that there are occasions where someone kills people because they think God told them to. I heard a guy say he bought yellow roses because God told him to and that was the girl's favorite color. I am not a judge of such things. But everyone has their experiences. I may share what I think of yours, but anything more than that is above my pay level, as they say.

Personally, I've never been completely satisfied by any explanation of someone having a personal relationship with God. Perhaps it is difficult to describe. It's like God talks to me but He doesn't really talk. Maybe He does, some time in some way? Regardless, there is something that is called a relationship. I just don't know what people mean when they say it. Personally, I pray and I give thanks. I've often pondered the song that has lyrics saying something like going to the garden while the dew is still on the roses. And, he walks with me and talks with me and tells me I am his own. And the joy we share as we tarry there no other has ever known. That's awesome. But I can only wish I could relate. I do believe it is different for all of us at different times.

This is not about relationship, but an experience. It is one that I always remember. In the mid-70's, I was with two other Christian brothers in a park. We met a cute woman about our age and began talking/flirting with her. She told us she was a witch. None of us said anything about us being Christian. She said, "You are Christians, I must leave." And she did.

When my son died, I went outside and hugged a tree. I prayed as sincerely as ever that God take me and let him live. I was serious and believed that could have happened. It didn't. I pray for things in my life and others and believe it makes a difference and hope it does. I'm not crazy in these regards. The only person who says God gave them the lottery numbers was a winner.

Allow me to quote Brierley again as he says this better than I could. "Throughout the journey, my quarrel has not been with the atheists, but with atheism. Having examined it from various angles, I have been unable to reconcile it with the world I find myself in. It's a world that is both mechanical and magical, beautiful yet broken, driven by natural laws yet teeming, just below the surface, with the presence of something altogether supernatural. In the end, Christianity still makes the most sense of life, the universe and everything." (Brierley 2017, 205-206)

"Only faith can guarantee the blessings that we hope for, or prove the existence of realities that are unseen. … It is by faith that we understand that the ages were created by a word from God, so that from the invisible the visible world came to be." (Hebrews 11:1-3)

If you haven't believed in God, I hope you consider reasons to do so. If you believe in God, I hope you consider that His interaction and revelation is given to us in the Bible. And, in the Bible you might find that Jesus is the son of God, who is God with the father and the holy spirit, in whom I believe and are therefore saved to live with God forever.

I believe in God, the Father, Son and Holy Spirit. I can't comprehend what is called the Trinity. I believe what is recorded for us in the bible. Christmas is about Christ. Jesus of Nazareth. I only know of these things from the Holy Bible. I believe the Bible is one way God reveals himself to us today by a recording of how he revealed himself to people in the past. It is one way as is natural revelation (beauty, science, etc.) and philosophy. There is sound history about some of this.

I know that there are questions about what is historical and about this and that and timelines and such. I am not going to go into all that stuff. I am going to say that from all that I know and have studied I still have as much (if not more) reason to believe in the Christian God than not. You may not agree, I respect that. If you are interested you can further study for yourself. There are tons of tomes on these subjects. I am no expert. I believe that I am open and will examine any new thing that challenges my belief. No body can examine everything, right?

I believe there is a God. I believe God created all that is. That includes me and you.. It is not necessary, but it makes sense that if God created people, he may interact with them. I believe that we learn much about that from the Old Testament. We learn more from the

New Testament. As a result of all I know I continue to believe in God the Father, Son, and Holy Spirit. Among all who claimed to be prophets and such, outside of the obviously crazies, only Jesus claimed to be the son of God and by other statements claiming to be God. I believe in his historical reality, his crucifixion and resurrection.

I believe there are many prophecies in the Old Testament that told of the virgin birth and Emmanuel (God with us). I believe the first disciples of Jesus suffered painful deaths at the hands of anti-Christians. I know people of other faiths have too. I believe that the Biblical theology of sin explains many of our problems. God is my creator and he cares for me. He gives me instructions. Have any of you parents not heard your child at one time say to you: You are not the boss of me? God is not our boss and we are not the boss of our children. The instruction we give is for their good because we love them. The instructions God provides us is because he loves us. There were writers contemporary with the New Testament writers. As far as I know there were none who challenged the writings about the crucifixion and resurrection of Jesus.

Christians have messed up in a lot of ways. (And also have other faiths,) That makes me sad. However, Christians have also been a source of good. Much of charitable good comes from Christians.

Everything I've written here expresses reasons why I believe in God. I hope you have found it interesting and maybe an encouragement to consider belief in God. And, I hope you have a Merry Christmas.

APOLOGETICS DON'T MEAN SAYING SORRY: AN ADDENDUM FOR CHRISTIANS

"**S**imply proclaim the Lord Christ holy in your hearts, and always have your answer ready for people who ask you the reason for the hope that you have" 1 Peter 3:15

It is Biblical; we are instructed to be prepared to share our reasons for belief. The totality of each person's reasons will not be the same as another's. Yet, some of the basics will be the same. If believing makes you happy and feel good, that is a good thing. God offers us peace beyond understanding and joy in the Lord. But your reason is surely more. After all, many atheists are happy. Christians should not apologize or be sorry for their faith. Apologetics has to do with developing reasons for the hope we have.

So, what is "apologetics?" The word "apologetic" is one of those words called a contranym. It has two meanings that are basically antithetical. To be apologetic can mean to be feeling sorry or expressing contrition. It can also mean putting up a defense (for something.) "Apologetics" is a specific use of the word. A description from Wikipedia follows.

"Apologetics is the religious discipline of defending religious doctrines through systemic argumentation and discourse. Early

Christian writers who defended their beliefs against critics and recommended their faith to outsiders were called Christian apologists. In 21st-century usage, apologetics is often identified with debates over religion and theology."

It seems to me that the main question here is why Christianity (instead of other beliefs that are theistic)? This is going beyond why I believe there is a God. Honestly, I have given only little serious study to other major religions. The one thing I've read is that no prophet or holy person in any religion has actually claimed to be God. In my reading of the Bible, I see many ways that Jesus did.

I think there are many good aspects to Buddhism and Hinduism and Islam. None of their prophets claimed to be God. Being repeatedly reincarnated or absorbed in to nirvana or such doesn't sound like entering the kingdom of God in heaven.

Having solid reasons for our belief and faith is also good for supporting us in times of trials and tribulations. When you find your faith being seriously challenged, you are encouraged to pray, talk to others you trust who may help, read scripture. If you have reasons for belief in your head, you will reflect on them. It is another source of help.

If you want to build on extra-Biblical reasons to believe, meaning history, philosophy, and science, I think there are some good books to read in the bibliography. I encourage Brierley (2017), Flew (2007), Lewis (1952), and Josh McDowell's Evidence that Demands a Verdict: Historical Evidences for the Christian Faith – 2 Volume Set.

May we all grow in the faith and ability to share our faith. May we love each other and those of other faiths without sacrificing the truth. God bless and Godspeed.

BIBLIOGRAPHY

Al-Khalili, Jim. *"Everything and Nothing: What is nothing?"* https://youtu.be/rkPv8zApeeo

Axe, Douglas. 2016. *Undeniable: How biology confirms our intuition that life is designed.* New York: Harper Collins Publishers

Brierley, Justin. 2017. *Unbelievable? Why, after ten years of talking with atheists, I'm still a Christian.* London: Society for Promoting Christian Knowledge

Dawkins, Richard. 2006. *The God Delusion.* New York: Houghton Mifflin Company

Feser, Edward. 2008. *The Last Superstition: A refutation of the new atheism.* South Bend, IN: St. Augustine's Press

Flew, Antony (Ed.). 1964. *Body, Mind, and Death: From Hippocrates to Gilbert Ryle on the question "What is consciousness?"* London: The Macmillan Company

Flew, Antony. 2007. *There is a God: How the world's most notorious atheist changed his mind.* New York: Harper One

Furst, Charles. 1979. *Origins of the Mind: Mind-Brain Connections.* New Jersey: Prentice-Hall, Inc.

Geisler, Norman L. and Turek, Frank. 2004. *I Don't Have Enough Faith to Be an Atheist.* Wheaton, IL: Crossway

Gleick, James. 1978. *Chaos: Making a new science.* New York: Viking Penguin Inc.

Gribbin, John. 2011. *Alone in the Universe: Why our planet is unique.* Hoboken, NJ: John Whiley & Sons, Inc.

Groothuis, Douglas. 2011. *Christian Apologetics: A Comprehensive Case for Biblical Faith.* Downers Grove, IL: Intervarsity Press

Hawking, Stephen. 2018. *Brief Answers to the Big Questions.* New York: Bantam Books

Hawking, Stephen. 2001. *The Universe in a Nutshell.* New York: Bantam Books

Hawing, Stephen and Mlodinow, Leonard. 2012. *The Grand Design.* New York: Bantam Books

Harding, Fred. *Stephen Hawking and the Divine Author: The day Hawking found God but couldn't believe his eyes.* United Kingdom

Hitchens, Christopher. 2007. *God is Not Great: How Religion Poisons Everything.* New York: Twelve

Hitchens, Peter. 2010. *The Rage Against God: How atheism led me to faith.* Grand Rapids, MI: Zondervan

Keathley, Kenneth, Stump, J. B. and Aguirre, Joe (Eds.). 2017. *Old-Earth or Evolutionary Creation? Discussing Origins with Reasons to Believe and Biologos.* Downers Grove, IL: InterVarsity Press

Keller, Timothy. 2018. *The Reason for God: Belief in an age of skepticism.* New York: Penguin Books

Krauss, Lawrence M. 2012. *A Universe from Nothing: Why there is something rather than nothing.* New York: Free Press

Kreeft, Peter and Tacelli, K. 1994. *Handbook of Christian Apologetics: Hundreds of Answers to Crucial Questions.* Downers Grove, IL: Intervarsity Press

Leisola, Matti and Witt, Jonathan. 2018. *Heretic: One Scientist's Journey from Darwin to Design.* Seattle: Discovery Institute

Lewis, C. S. 1940. *The Problem of Pain.* New York: Harper One

Lewis, C.S. 1952. *Mere Christianity*. New York: Harper One

Lewis, C. S. 1955. *Surprised by Joy.* New York: Harper One

Lewis, C. S. 1970. *God in the Dock*. Grand Rapids, MI: Wm. B. Eerdmans Publishing Co.

Pope, Kenneth S. and Singer, Jerome L. (Eds) 1978. *The Stream of Consciousness: Scientific Investigations into the Flow of Human Experience.* New York: Plenum Press

Powell, Diane Hennacy, M.D. 2009. *The ESP Enigma: The scientific case for psychic phenomena.* New York: Walker Publishing Company, Inc.

Rasmussen, Joshua. 2019. *How Reason Can Lead to God: A philosopher's bridge to faith.* Downers Grove Illinois: IVP Academic

Ross, Hugh. 1983. *The Creator and the Cosmos: How the greatest scientific discoveries of the century reveal God.* Colorado Springs, CO: Navpress

Ross, Hugh. 2014. *Navigating Genesis: A Scientist's Journey through Genesis 1 -11.* Covina, CA: Reasons to Believe

Ross, Hugh. 2016. *Improbable Planet: How Earth Became Humanity's Home.* Grand Rapids, MI: Baker Books

Schaeffer, Francis. 1976. *How Should We Then Live.* Wheaton: Crossway

Schaeffer, Frank. 2014. *Why I am an Atheist Who Believes in God: How to give love, create beauty and find peace.* Salisbury, M.A.: Regina Orthodox Press

Schroeder, Gerald L. 2001. *The Hidden Face of God: Science Reveals the Ultimate Truth.* New York: Touchstone

Schwartz, Gary E., Ph.D. 2006. *The G.O.D. Experiments: How science is discovering god in everything, including us.* New York: Atria Books

Stump, J.B. (Gen. Ed.). 2017. *Four Views on Creation, Evolution, and Intelligent Design.* Grand Rapids, MI: Zondervan

Varghese, Roy Abraham. 2003. *The Wonder of the World: A Journey from Modern Science to the Mind of God.* Fountain Hills, AZ: Tyr Publishing

Wilker, Benjamin and Witt, Jonathan. 2006. *A Meaningful World: How the arts and sciences reveal the genius of nature.* Downers Grove, IL: InterVarsity Press

www.ingramcontent.com/pod-product-compliance
Lightning Source LLC
Chambersburg PA
CBHW051231120626
46547CB00013B/1596